photo
GRAPHICS

photo GRAPHICS

PHIL BRODATZ

AMPHOTO
American Photographic Book Publishing
An Imprint of Watson-Guptill Publications
New York, New York 10036

First published in New York, New York, by American Photographic
Book Publishing: an imprint of Watson-Guptill Publications, a
division of Billboard Publications, Inc., 1515 Broadway, New York,
NY 10036.

Library of Congress Cataloging in Publication Data

Brodatz, Phil.
   PhotoGRAPHICS: a workshop in high-contrast darkroom
techniques.

   Includes index.
   1. Photography—Special effects. 2. Photography—
Processing. I. Title.
TR148.B692.   770'.28   81-10970
ISBN 0-8174-5417-9   AACR2

Manufactured in the United States of America
First printing, 1981
1 2 3 4 5 6 7 8 9/86 85 84 83 82 81

All photographs for which no other credit is given are by the author.

To Lillian

ACKNOWLEDGMENTS

A project of this size and scope doesn't just happen. It takes a number of good friends to administer large doses of help and encouragement.

This is my opportunity to say "Thank You" to Judy Wolfson, Dennis Harkins, Julie Grodenchik, and Rusty Morris.

To Ernest Seemann of E. A. Seemann Publishing Inc. Thank you for permission to use the illustration of Ernest Hemingway.

To Josefina Inclán for her inspiration to creativity.

Contents

Introduction

Graphics is a form of printed or artistic communications often executed in a bold, dramatic manner. This book is a guide to the production of graphic images by photographic methods — or *photoGRAPHICS*. Starting with the photogram, the simplest of images, the reader will go through intermediate stages to the most complex *photoGRAPHIC* images such as color posterizations.

Each chapter has an introduction to aid the reader in grasping the process, followed by complete instructions for performing it. Both theoretical and practical information on materials, practical tips, and suggestions for inventing some variations of your own are presented.

In this book the Eastman Kodak Company brand names for films, paper, and chemistry are used. These products are universally known and are considered industry standards. Many manufacturers make comparable and competitive products. Feel free to use whatever brand you wish, as long as it is equivalent.

Careful use of this book will give you an understanding of line, continuous tone, and halftone. You will also learn to master Kodalith, an extreme high-contrast film, and will acquire the ability to prepare both negative and positive films by a number of means. In addition, mastering the techniques of registration will enable you to print two or more films on one sheet of paper in sequence and with precision.

Think of a printed page as black and white. The paper is white with black ink impressed on it. The type is solid black, but what is the gradation of a photograph? To find out, place a strong magnifying glass on a printed photograph. Under the glass, the picture becomes a myriad of individual dots, each of which is solid black. The illusion of gradation is achieved by representing the light tones as small dots, the middle tones as larger dots, the dark gray and black tones as large almost-square shapes, and the largest as masses formed by many dots.

Three processes, *line*, *continuous tone*, and *halftone*, are crucial to understanding *photoGRAPHICS*. *Line* expresses that image which is wholly black and white, an image without gradation. Line represents the highest contrast.

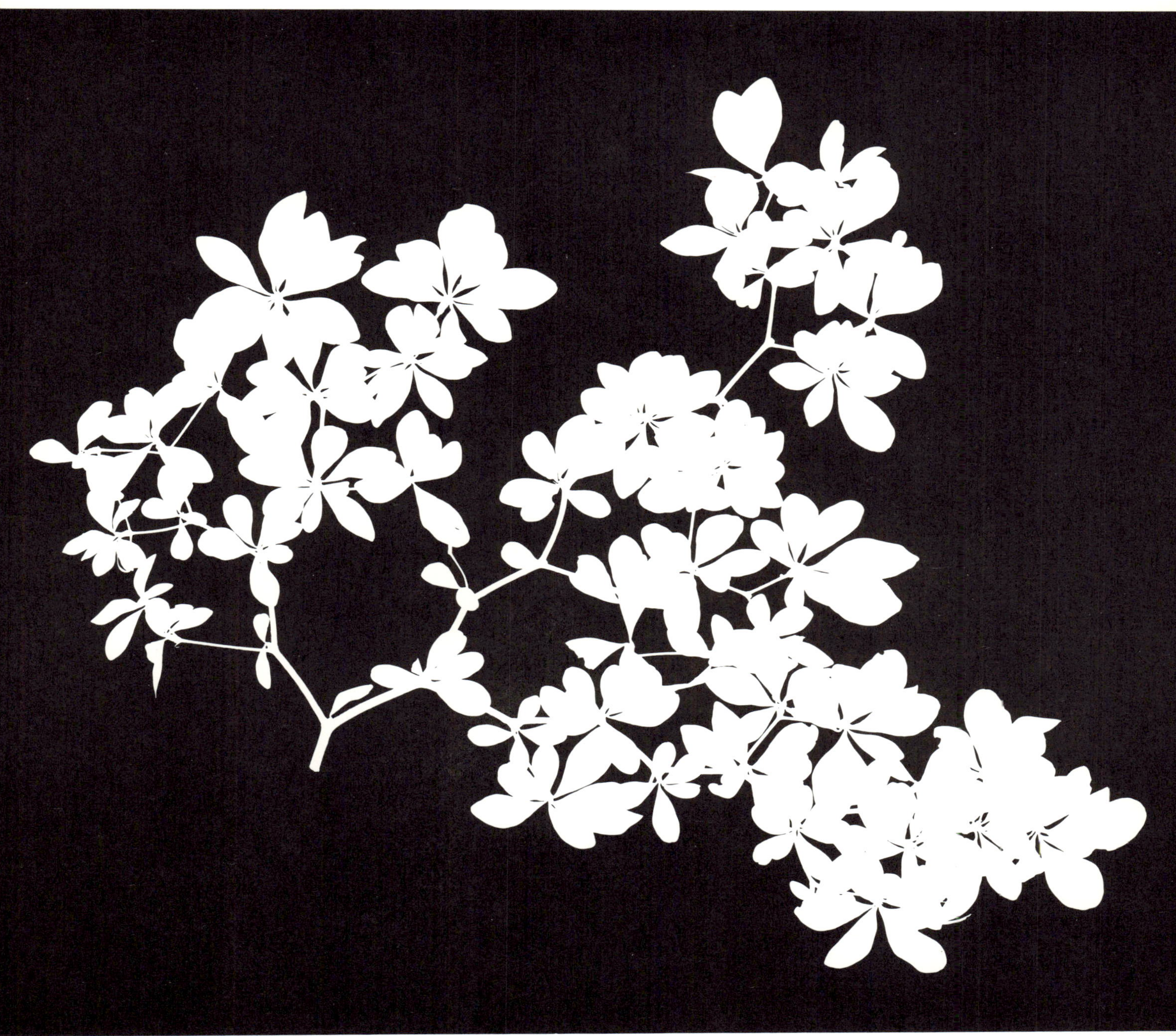

A photogram of a tree branch.

At the other end of the scale is the form of photography that we normally practice. The image in a photographic print or negative is composed of many, many shades of gray. It is called *continuous tone*.

The ink-printed image of a photograph is called a *halftone*. It is created by photographing a continuous-tone image through a halftone screen onto a sheet of line film. This results in the dots that visually correspond to the tones of the original picture.

Part One:
HIGH-CONTRAST TECHNIQUES

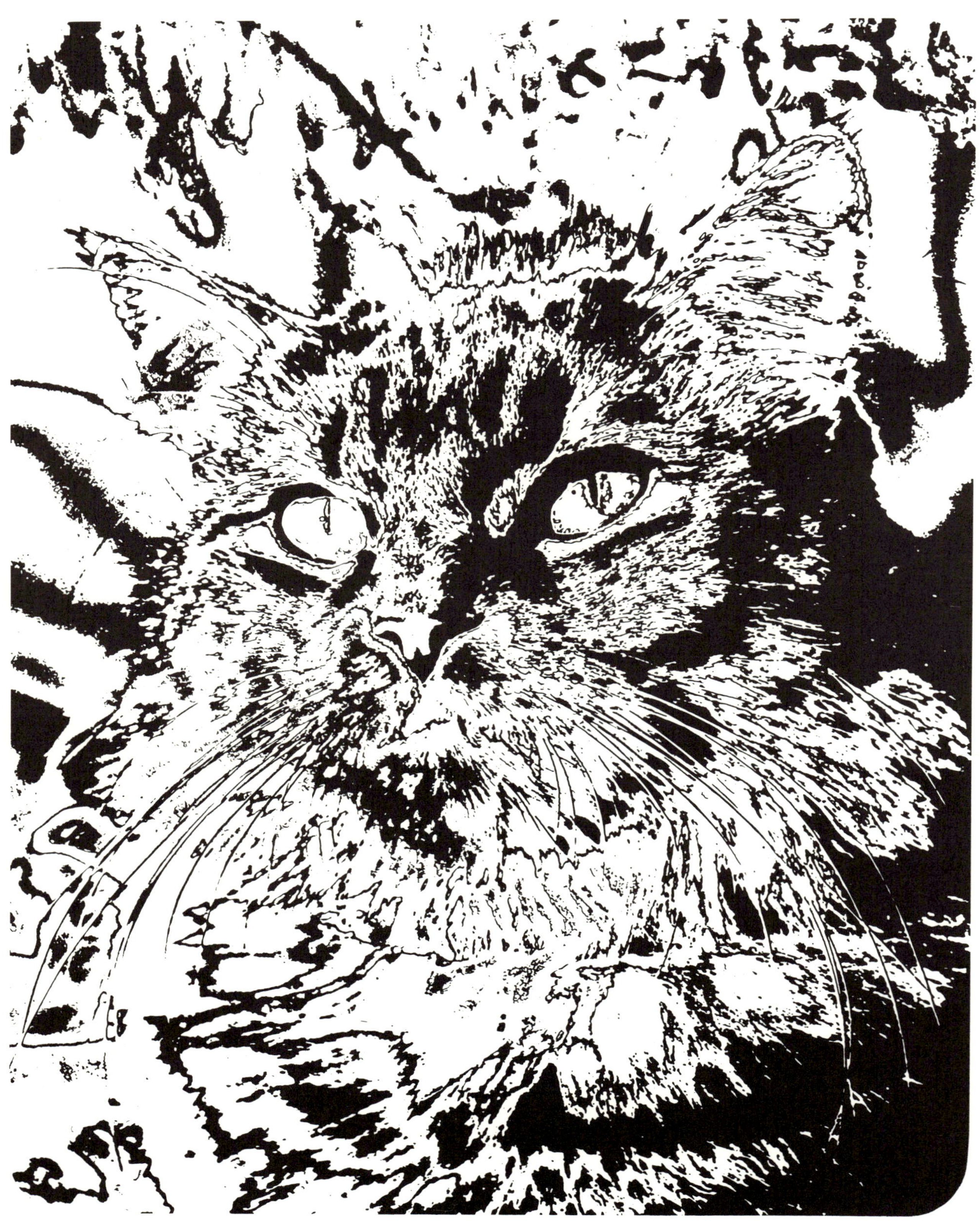

An Introduction to Line

Images composed only of black and white—whether in lines or solid areas—are referred to as *line* images. The basic example of a line image is a *photogram*, which in its simplest form is a two-tone photographic print. The first photogram you will make is a high-contrast black-and-white print. The white will be clear and the black will be solid.

The second will be black, white, and one tone of gray. This exercise will make you aware of the multi-tone character of the film and paper that you normally use. You will learn to control exposure and processing to make this material behave like a line image.

Place an object between a sheet of photographic paper and a light source. Turn the light on and off. Process the paper.

This is actually all you need to do to produce a photogram. It is step one in basic photography and will open the door to a world of shapes and forms to study and play with.

Supplies and Equipment

- Enlarger
- Safelight
- Processing trays
- Enlarging paper
- Dektol paper developer
- Stop bath
- Fixer (acid hardening)
- Hypo clearing agent
- Tongs
- Wash

Instructions

Use your enlarger as a light source. Place the sheet of enlarging paper on the baseboard, and position the object on the sheet of paper.

Check your light source to see that it is high enough to cover the paper. Be sure that the paper is centered within the area of the light. To do this, put the red safelight disc in position under the lens, and turn the enlarger light on. If you do not have a disc, you can center your work by marking the baseboard with guidelines. I suggest that you use strips of white or tan masking tape. Because they are light

BLACK-AND-WHITE TONES

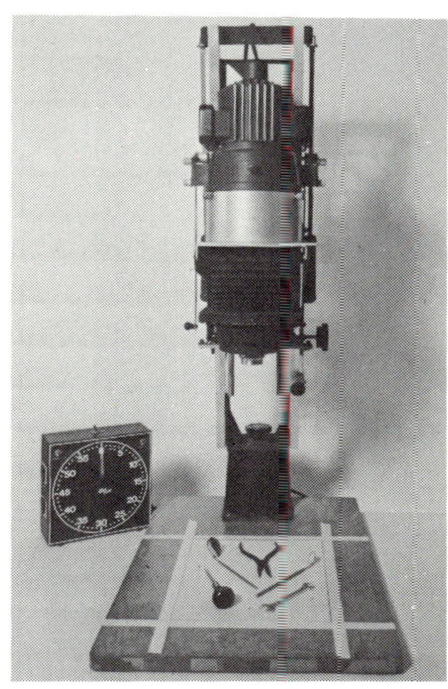

An enlarger is a convenient light source for photograms. The use of tape on the baseboard will help position the paper.

in color they will be easy to see in the dark. They can easily be removed or repositioned without damaging the baseboard.

To start with, set the aperture on the enlarging lens to $f/8$ or $f/11$ and your timer for 3 seconds. After the exposure, process the paper as though you had just made an enlargement.

Read the instructions packed with the paper, and follow them carefully. (Note that the instructions may differ somewhat from those given below.) Process the paper under safelight conditions:

Dektol developer, 1:2*	1½	min.
Stop bath	30	sec.
Fixer (acid hardening)	5	min.
Hypo clearing agent**	2	min.
Wash	5	min.
Dry		

*The proportion for the developer is one part stock solution to two parts water.

**An optional Hypo clearing agent is used to shorten the wash and help preserve the print.

You have just made a trial run-through for printing. This first print should be examined to see (1) if the white area is clear with no grayness, and to determine (2) if the black area is black — very black — or thin and grayish.

If the white is clear, it indicates that the light intensity and exposure time were just about right.

If the black is truly black, it shows that the intensity of light and exposure time are correct.

If the white area shows some grayness, there was either too much light or exposure time.

Before you make another print, set up a control using a gray-scale test strip. Making a series of test strips will help you determine the paper speed and, with a little experience, its contrast. This will show you the printing qualities of an unfamiliar brand or type of photo paper. To get a feeling for an enlarger or contact printer, it also helps to make a series of test strips. These test the time in seconds that it takes to produce a black and selected gray tones.

To understand *posterization* it is necessary to comprehend that *continuous tone* moves from light to dark in smooth, delicate shadings. A gray scale demonstrates that grays can be broken into time segments. At right is a picture of an 11-step scale, a representation of the number of grays that can be made by a film or a paper.

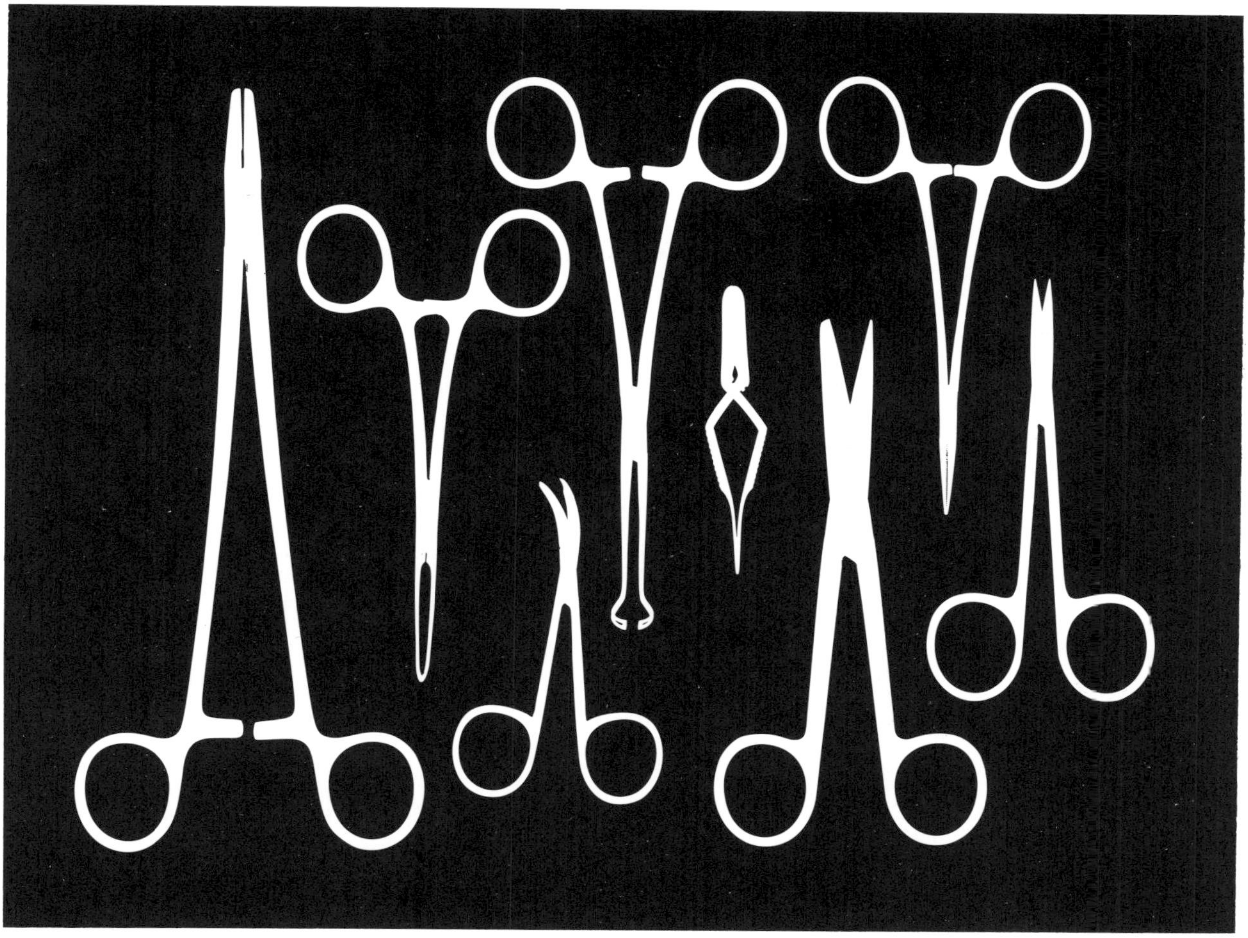

Photograms achieve a bold graphic image without the use of a camera.
Only light, film or paper, and a selection of objects are required.

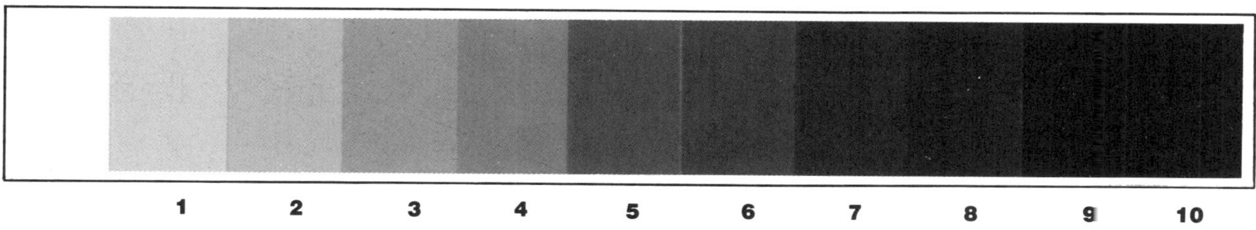

A gray-scale test strip. The white step was covered from the very
beginning and, therefore, received no exposure. The numbers indicate the
seconds of exposure for each successive step.

Examine a photograph, looking for the steps of gray that comprise the image. If there are four or five major tones making up the whole image, think in terms of extracting each tone. Then, reassemble each one as a gray value from the steps of the gray scale. If you want to produce a very bright, colorful print, you can reassemble these values as color hues on color paper, or they may be reassembled as color transparencies, or even as color negatives.

PREPARING A TEST STRIP

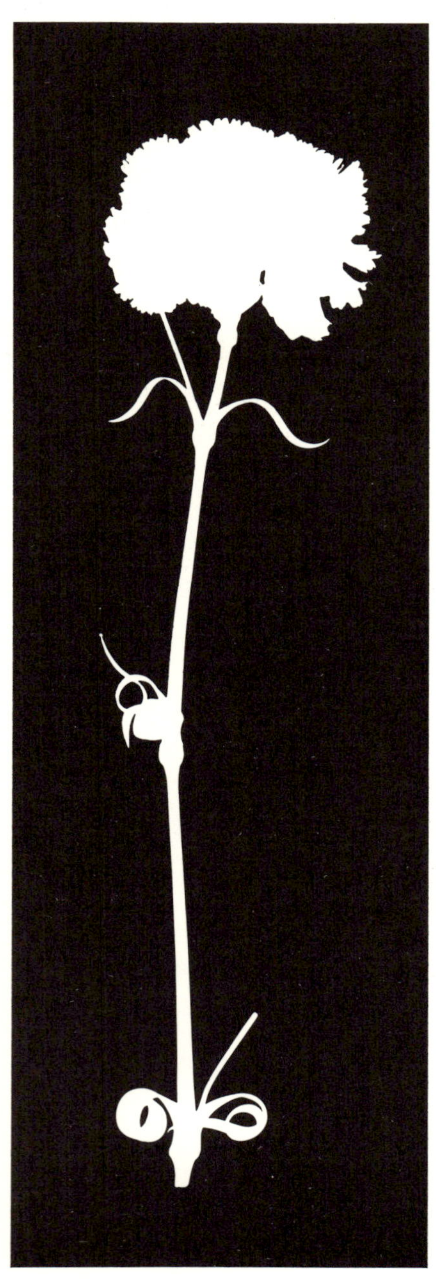

Materials

Enlarging paper

Tape

Cardboard

Instructions

Cut a strip of enlarging paper measuring approximately 2″ × 10″ (5 cm × 25 cm). Tape it to the baseboard. Hold a piece of cardboard in your hand. Be sure it is large enough to cover the test strip. Then set the enlarger lens at $f/8$ or $f/11$. Set the timer for 1 second.

Expose the test strip ten times at 1-second intervals. For the first exposure, cover about one inch at the left end. After the first exposure, slide the cardboard to the right in 1-inch (3-cm) segments. Ideally, the eleven steps of the test strip should be separate and distinct from each other.

When using the enlarger as a light source, you will need to use enlarging paper, because of the enlarger's higher speed. However, if you chose another light source delivering more light than the enlarger/lens system, try contact paper, instead. The slower speed of the contact paper will offset the brighter light source.

If the test strip goes from white to black in 3 or 4 seconds, there will not be enough time for control or to get strips of gray between the white and black. To increase the time, we need to reduce the light intensity. To do this, raise the enlarger head, or close the lens aperture one f-stop. Closing the aperture is a more precise, easily repeated control. By changing the aperture from $f/8$ to $f/11$, we halve the amount of light. It will, therefore, take double the time to obtain the same value of gray at each stop.

For example, assuming our original test strip produced black at 3 seconds with $f/8$: move to $f/11$ for black in 6 seconds or to $f/16$ for black in 12 seconds.

To get a maximum black, allow 10 to 12 seconds. From now on, set your aperture and column height to these positions. It would be wise to mark the column in some way and record this data. Remember that if you change the paper, the enlarger height, or the light intensity, you should rerun a test strip to avoid poor or inaccurate results.

As a starting point, I suggest using the enlarger as a controlled light source. You can free yourself from the restriction of a straight-down overhead light by substituting a small flashlight, or a high-intensity desk lamp; these can be aimed at your object layout from any direction.

Now that you can control the mechanical portion of the procedure, it's time to turn to aesthetic concerns. Begin with such simple objects as keys, paper clips, flowers, and spaghetti, and build toward more interesting possibilities. Noting the following should stimulate you and give you further ideas. When an object intercepts a single light source, a shadow is cast. Depending on the angle of the light variations, the shadow will assume different shapes and sizes. What we are actually recording is a shadow of the object, not a picture of it. You are not limited to head-on, noontime light. As you walk down the street in late afternoon, look at the shadow you cast. Watch it flat on the ground; watch it climb a wall. These variations can be recreated with different objects on your tabletop at home. The possibilities are almost endless.

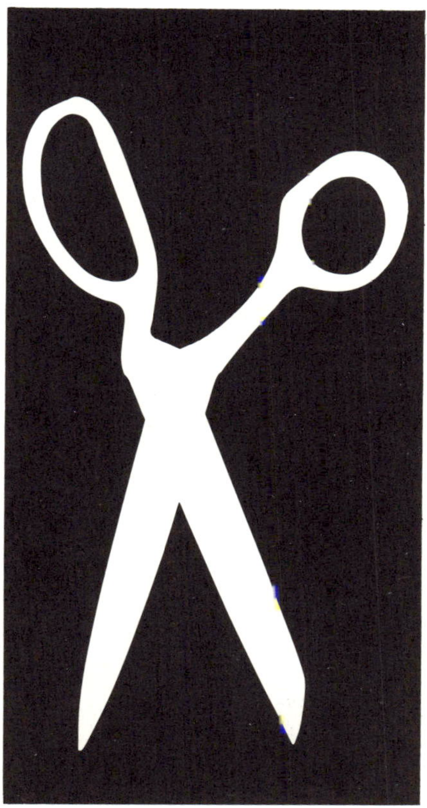

Any object is suitable for a photogram, which has a myriad of uses, from simple decoration to symbols on labels.

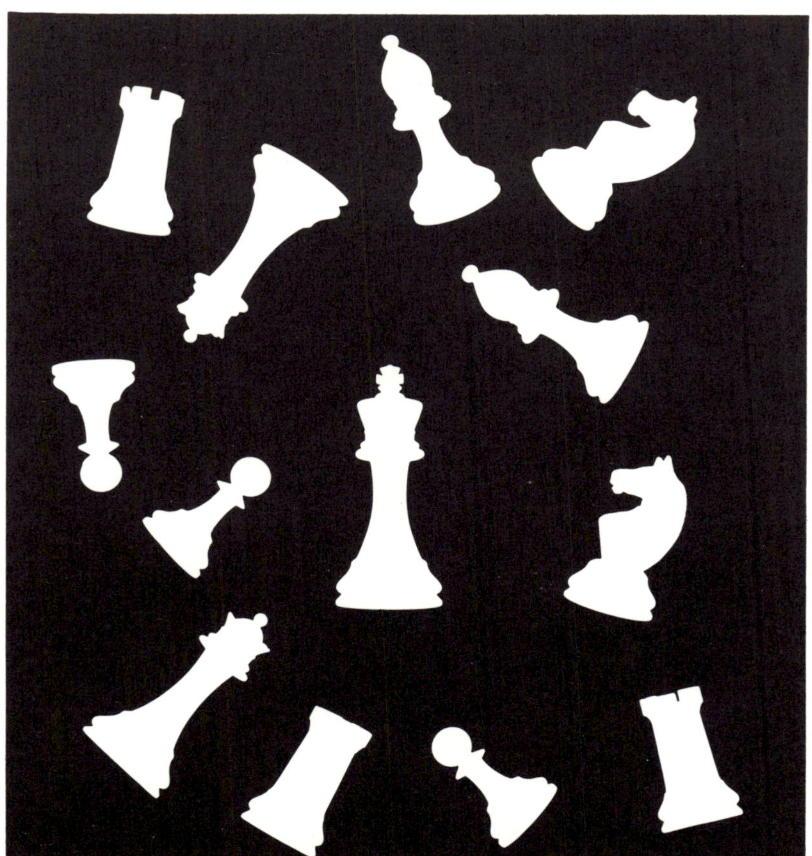

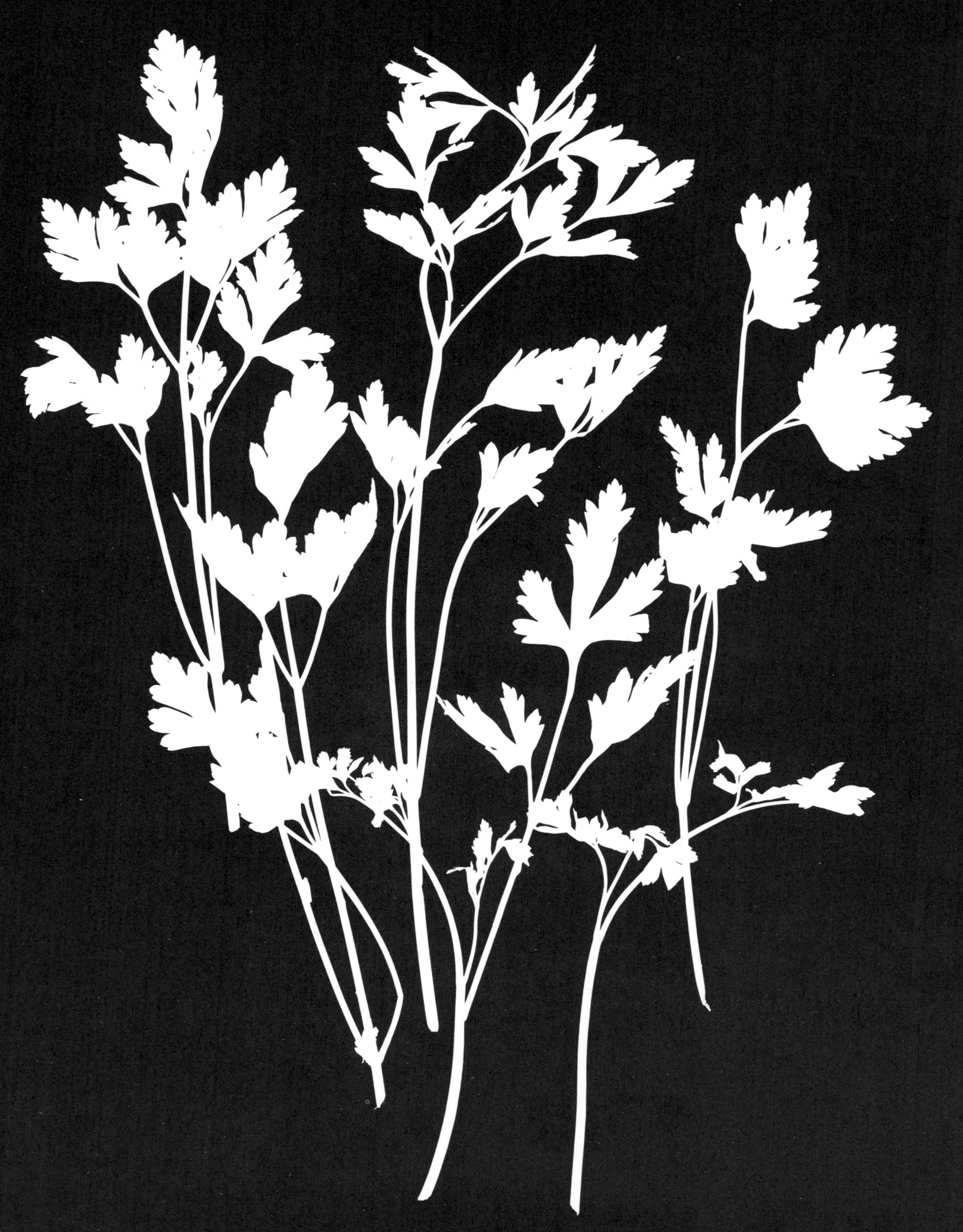

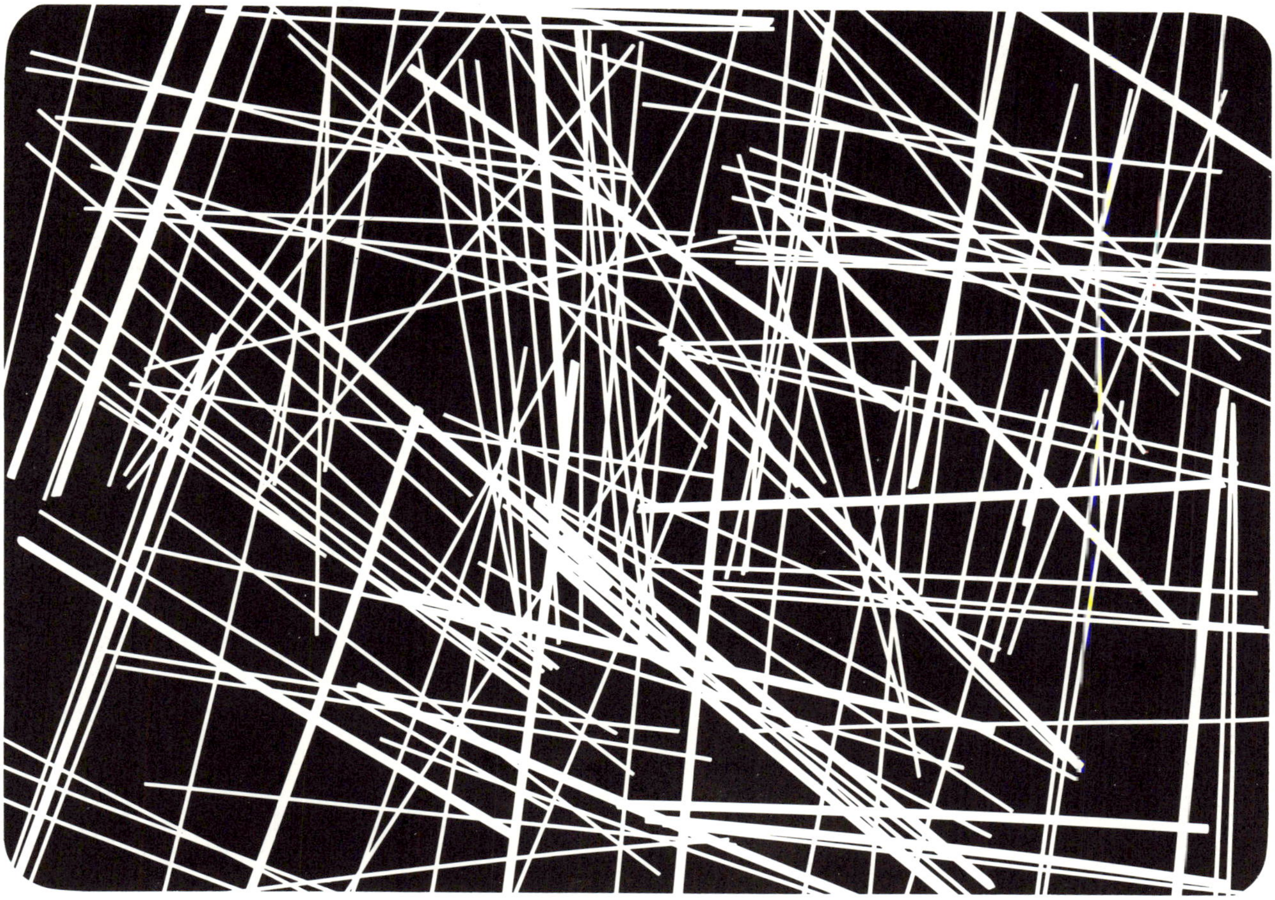

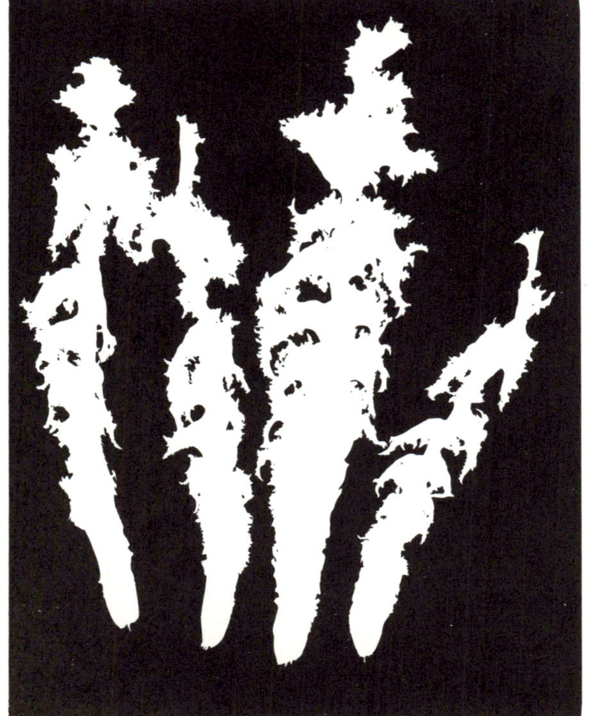

Photograms provided the decoration for the interior of a new building. The inspiration for the design motif was the supermarket. The multi-crossed lines are various sizes of spaghetti; the vegetables are escarole and parsley.

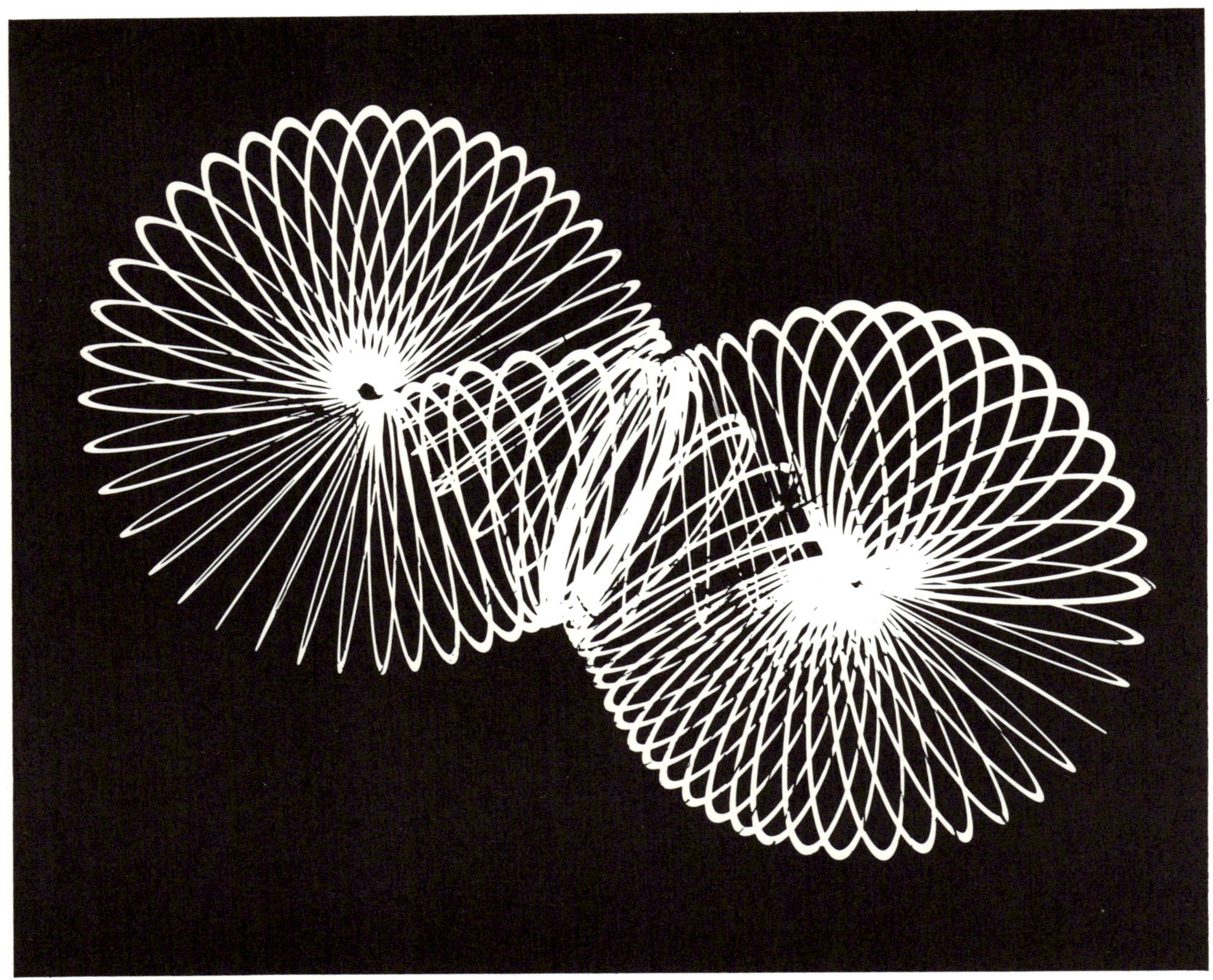

Above. *Such items as this coiled-spring Slinky toy can provide highly pleasing design variations.*

Right. *An evergreen twig can provide a winter design. You can make the photogram in black and white and then color the twig green with felt markers. Or you can use a green-base photo paper, which is available from some suppliers. Another alternative is to use color photo paper and print a background of the desired hue (see Chapter 8 for instructions).*

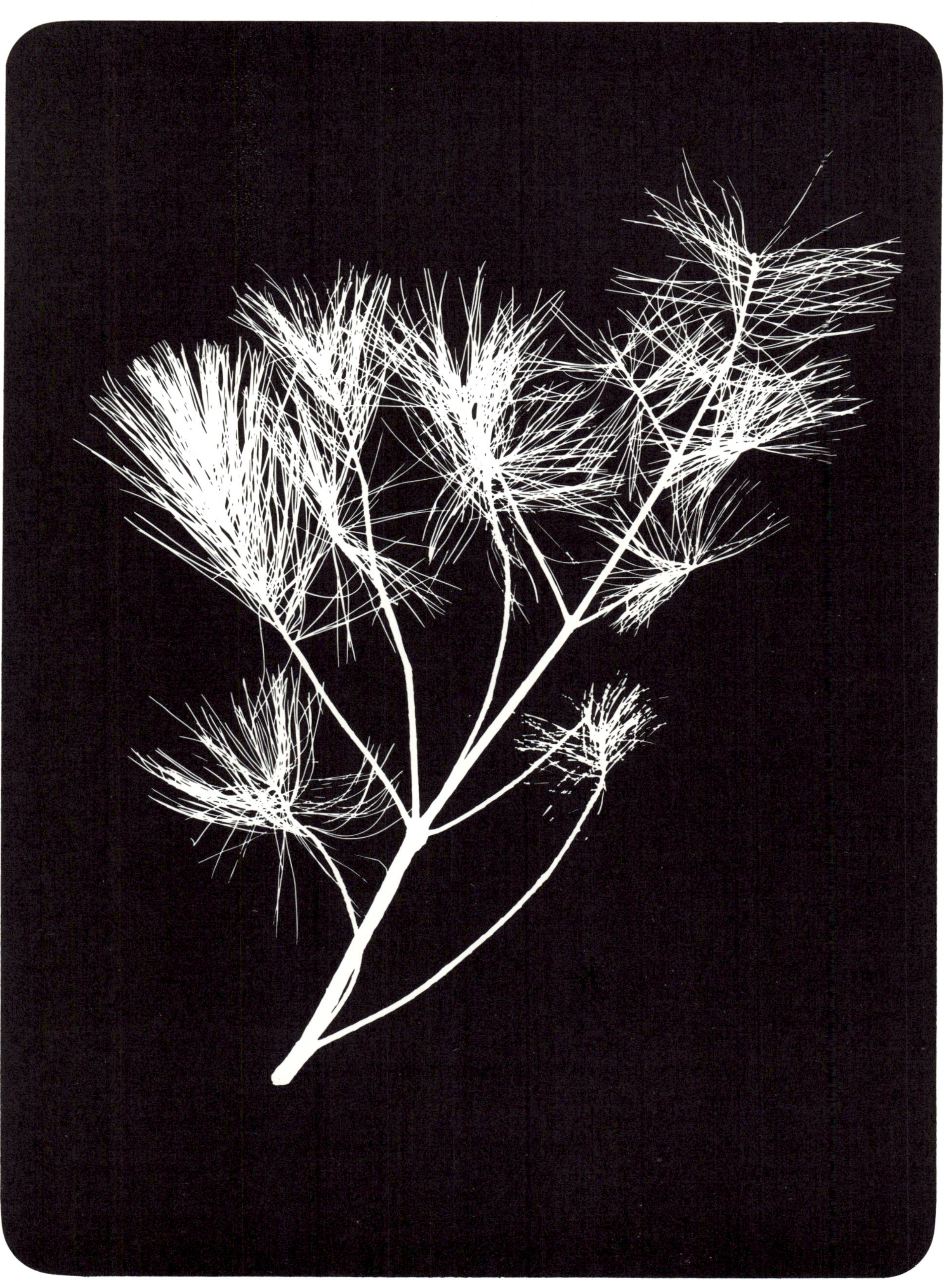

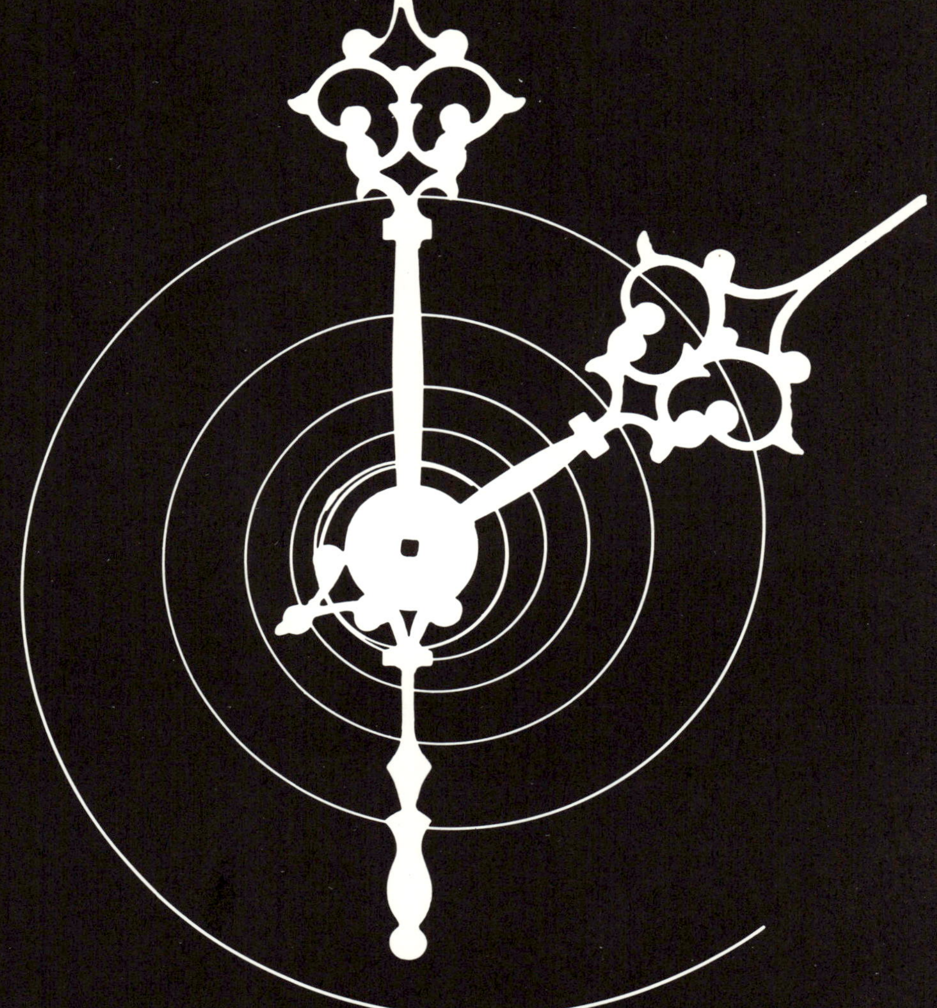
En las Agujas del Tiempo
Josefina Inclán

By this time, you have mastered the preparation of a control test strip and of a black-and-white print. The next adventure is to produce a print comprised of three tones—black, white, and gray. Go back to the enlarger. Arrange a series of objects on the enlarging paper. Select one tone from your gray-scale test strip, and note the number of seconds it takes to produce this tone. (Refer to the test strip on page 17.)

Assume that we select a middle gray that requires a 5-second exposure. (We know that it takes 10 seconds to reach a black.)

Procedure

Expose for 5 seconds.

Remove some objects.

Expose for 5 additional seconds.

Process the paper.

If you have followed the procedure correctly, a 10-second black will be placed in some areas, even though it has taken two exposures to do so. You will have placed a 5-second gray in the areas from which you removed some objects, retaining a white tone in the balance. White is the tone produced in each area remaining covered for the full exposure time.

Our two trial exposures were 5 + 5 seconds. These can be varied as we please:

2 + 8 sec.   or   3 + 7 sec.   or   4 + 6 sec.

6 + 4 sec.   or   7 + 3 sec.   or   8 + 2 sec.

or even 1 + 9 sec.

A total of 10 seconds makes black. The shorter exposure range is our control of gray; the shorter the first exposure, the darker the gray. This is because the paper will receive a longer exposure after the objects have been removed.

As simple as these exercises appear to be, your judgment, compositional ability, and imagination can come into play to create innumerable variations. Some of your prints will be good; some will be excellent. Compare your prints, and try to determine why some have come out better than others.

CREATING A PHOTOGRAM IN BLACK, WHITE, AND ONE GRAY TONE

Left. *Photogram created for the cover of a book entitled,* In the Eye of Time. *The juxtaposition of old clock hands and a wire spring cleverly depicts the content.*

Good composition will help improve the quality of your results. Compose your chosen objects within the area of the sheet, and consider the position of the cast shadow. Train yourself to "see" the effect each object makes in casting its shadow. Finally, be adventurous and imaginative in your selection of objects. Translucent objects, such as pieces of lucite and marbles, make especially interesting subjects. The light refracts in unusual ways, producing surprising shapes and patterns. A pencil flashlight, taped so that only a small amount of light is emitted, is particularly useful for manipulating the light.

An Introduction to Kodalith

Kodalith is a high-contrast film, especially created for the printing industry. In a single exposure, it retains the white and black tones and loses the gray. However, Kodalith is a basic silver halide emulsion and can be controlled and manipulated to produce very effective photographic images. At one end of the scale, Kodalith film processed in Kodalith developer is an extreme-contrast, black-and-clear film. At the other, Kodalith film processed in diluted D-76 developer can produce full-scale tone negative or positive films.

The film's special advantage is its clarity of film base. With other regular films there is some degree of *base density* (the amount of grayness we perceive). The more extended the developing time, or the older the film, the

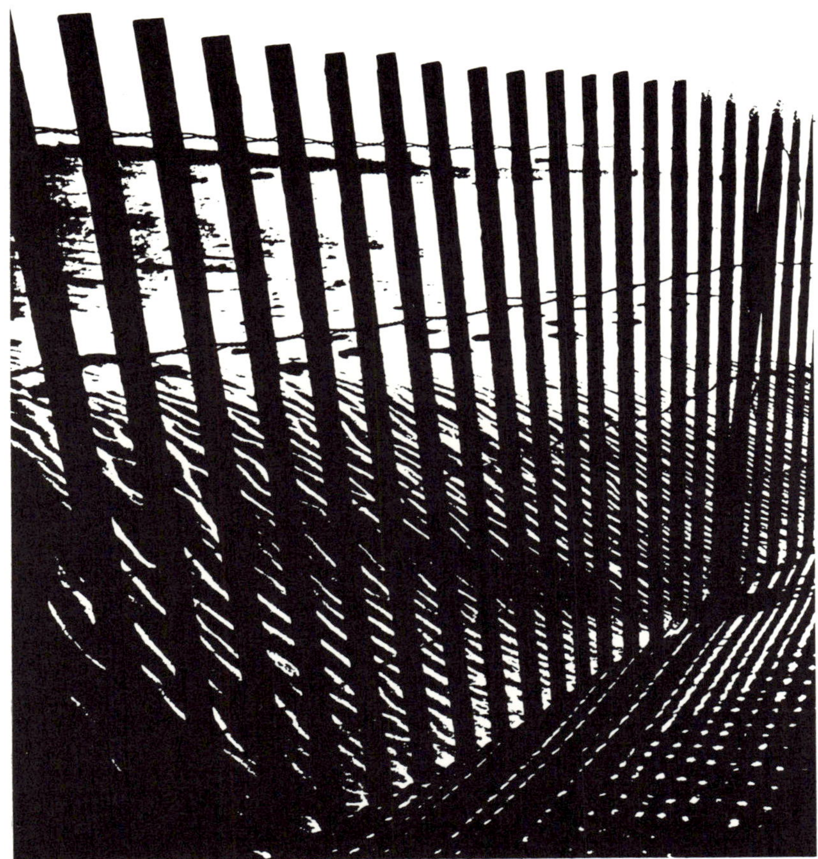

"Snow Fences" is a straightforward enlargement from a black-and-white negative onto Kodalith film. The Kodalith creates this photoGRAPHIC effect.

more apparent this fogginess will be. Kodalith base, on the other hand, is perfectly clear. This feature makes it suitable for producing positive tone films to be used on illuminators (or light tables). It can also be used to produce texture screens and for various degrees of masking. In addition, Kodalith has sufficient speed to be used as a camera film and is ideal for contact or projection printing. All in all, it is a most versatile photographic material.

When you place the Kodalith film on the easel for exposure, put a sheet of black matte paper under the film. This will prevent *halation*, the flaring of the image caused by reflected light. If the Kodalith is exposed on a white surface there is a distinct possibility that the exposing light will pass through the film and be reflected back, thereby distorting the image. The matte black paper will prevent this from happening.

USING KODALITH

Supplies and equipment

An image (black-and-white, color negative, or color slide)

Kodalith Ortho Sheet Film, 4″ × 5″ (10 cm × 13 cm)

Kodalith developer, A and B

Stop bath

Fixer (acid hardening)

Hypo clearing agent

Safelight, 1A light red

Instructions

Step 1. Setup
Select an image you will enjoy working with while you master these techniques—a black-and-white negative, a color negative, or a color slide—and place it in the enlarger. Bring it into focus on the easel (use a scrap piece of white paper). Keep the projected image small: it should be no larger than about 3″ × 4″ (8 cm × 10 cm) to get it all on 4″ × 5″ (10 cm × 13 cm) film.

Under a red safelight (with the enlarger turned off), open the box of Kodalith and take out one sheet. Check to see that the emulsion side is facing up (this will be the lighter-colored side). To double-check, place the *tip* of your tongue to one corner of the film—the emulsion side will have a slightly salty taste. This check is advisable because Kodalith does not have identifying edge notches such as those in most sheet films.

Step 2. Exposure
Kodalith film is faster than enlarging paper, and so it will need less time or light intensity than that used with the paper for the photograms. Make a test strip, with the negative in place in the enlarger. Try $f/8$ at 1-second increments; five steps should be enough to enable you to select the correct exposure.

Throughout the test, keep one area completely covered. A 1-inch (3-cm) square of black masking tape works well for me. (Remember to remove the tape before processing.) This covered, unexposed area *must* be perfectly clear after processing. Any grayness indicates that something is wrong: unsafe safelight (for example, wattage is too powerful), overdevelopment, out-of-date film, or some other factor.

Step 3. Processing
Kodalith developer is available in both dry powder and liquid concentrate forms and consists of two solutions, A and B, which are to be combined in equal parts for use. The dry powder packets should be dissolved separately in one gallon (3.8 l) of water each to make working-strength solutions. Solutions will keep indefinitely in closed glass containers. The liquid concentrates are to be diluted to form working-strength solutions.

Do not mix equal parts of A and B together until just before you are ready to process the film. The mixed developer does not keep long in a tray, and developing, with its constant agitation, will accelerate its breakdown. Mix only as much developer as you need, and figure on a maximum effective time of about two hours. If the solution turns brown or darkens before then, discard it immediately and mix a fresh batch.

Use the developer at 68 F (20 C), or as close as possible. (If necessary, you can add a few ice cubes to lower the temperature without significantly affecting the developer.) Insert the film, emulsion side up, in the tray, and agitate continuously.

Processing-Time Table	
Developer	3 min.
Stop bath	30 sec.
Fixer	3 min.
Hypo clearing agent	1 min.
Wash	3 min.

To dry, use a squeegee on both sides of the film and then hang the film from one corner.

Opposite page. *"Cityscape" is a Kodalith print made directly from a color negative in the enlarger. The orange-brown base color of the negative did not cause problems in making this print.*

Below. *"Royal Poinciana," a Kodalith print, is an example of how graphic techniques work: we select the essence of form from nature but the final composition depends on aesthetic judgment.*

Developing for longer than 3 minutes is unnecessary. The image will start to be visible within 1 to 1½ minutes, appearing rapidly over a period of about 2½ minutes. The development rate decreases after that, and the image is fully developed within 3 minutes.

If the image contains very fine lines or details, reduce the total development time to 2½ minutes. You will know that the film was seriously overexposed if the image starts to show very quickly and then goes black. It can't be saved by pulling it immediately from the developer. Throw that print away and start again.

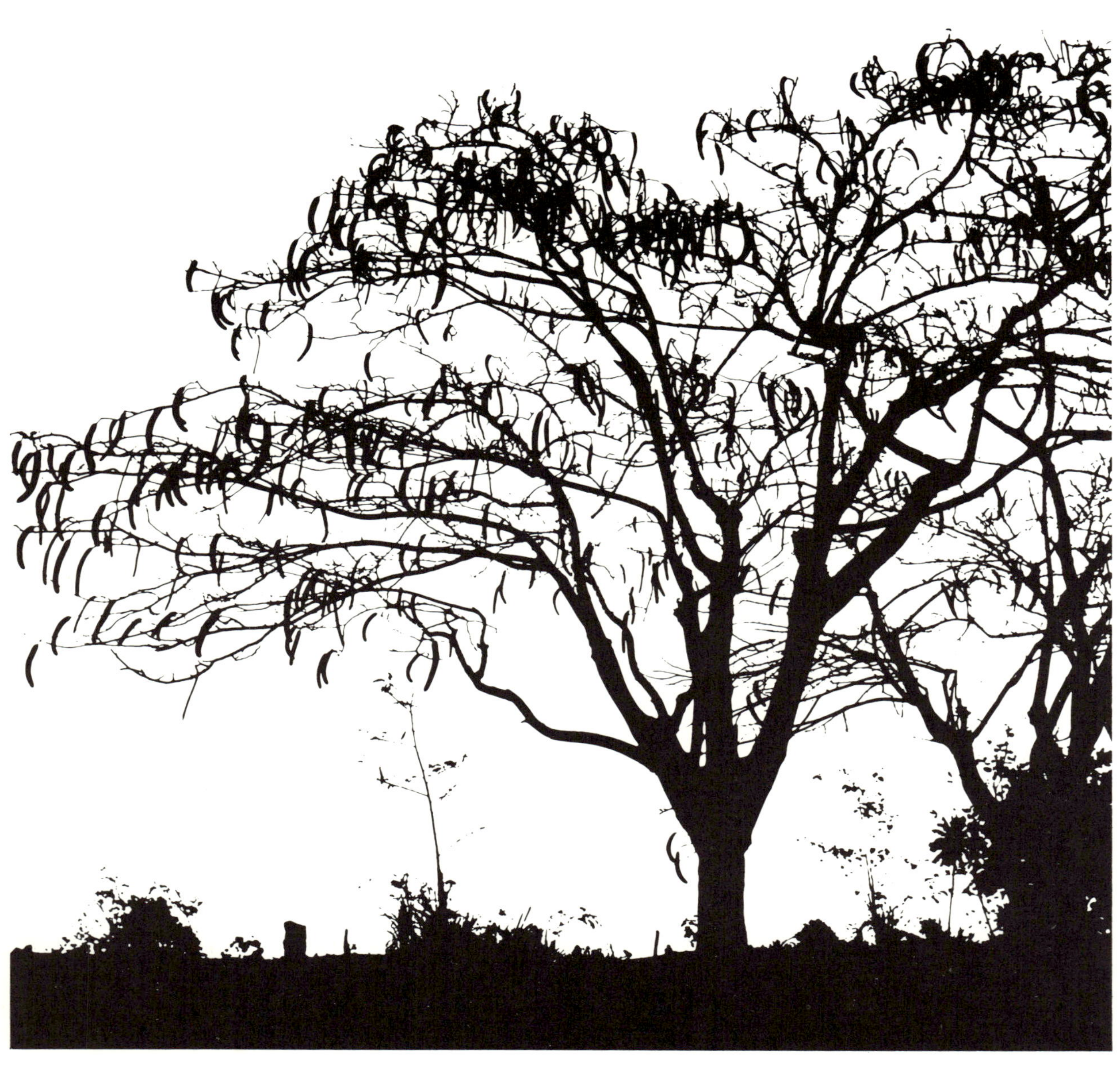

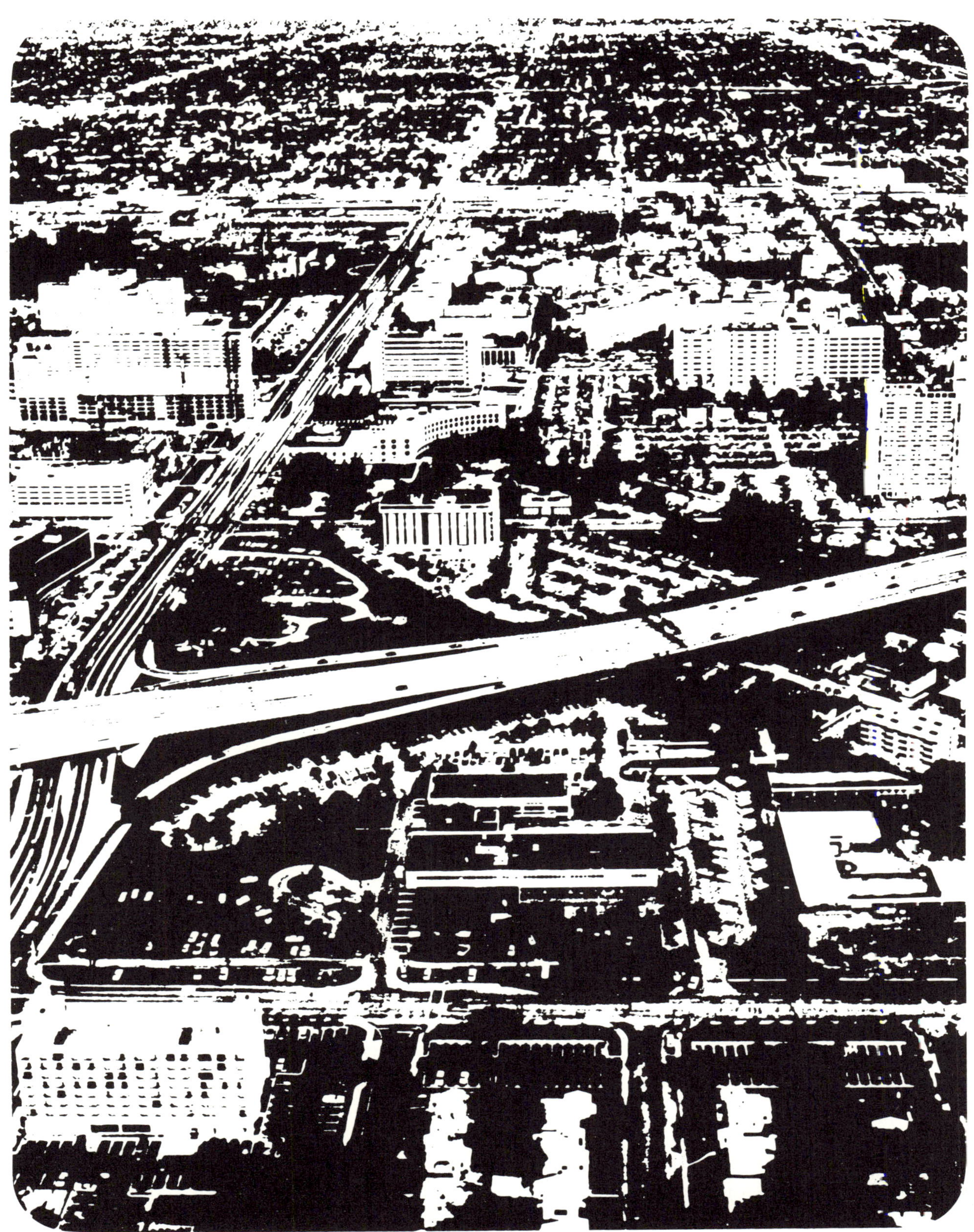

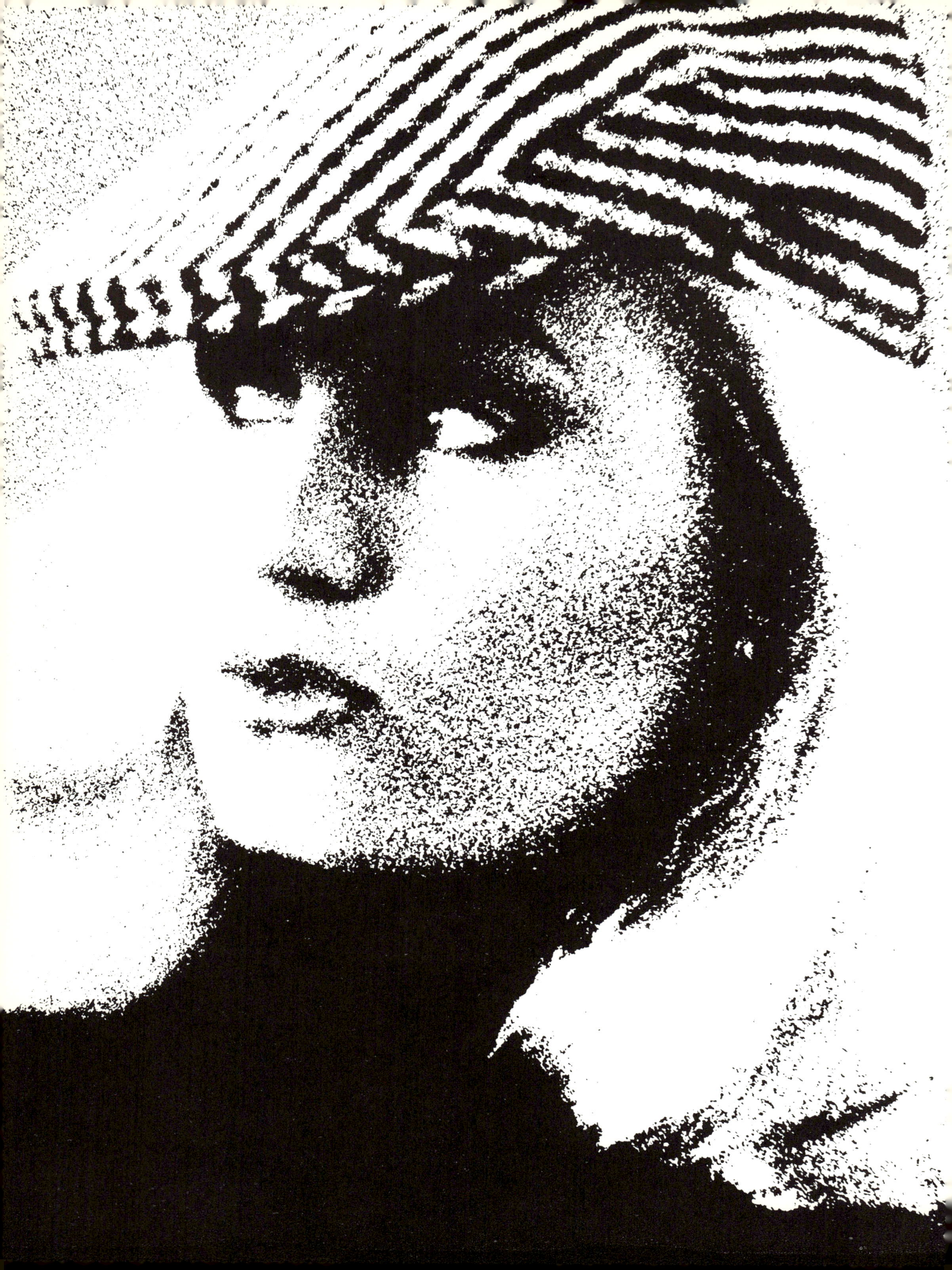

Go slowly. You must master the basics of Kodalith film before you can progress to more advanced techniques. Learning to expose and process it correctly is very important. Most of the illustrations in this book were produced from Kodalith images. Compare your results with these, so you'll have a clear idea of what you're aiming for.

Above all, standardize your procedures! If you vary the exposure or vary the developing time, or use old developer or other chemicals, you will have trouble repeating your results. If, however, your processing is standardized and consistent, you can learn to increase or decrease the exposure for *controlled* variations.

When you have finally produced a good Kodalith film image, you will be ready to take it to the next stage, as discussed in the section below. The image produced is called an *abstraction* —the gray zones have been deleted, and it is hoped that the high-contrast result will retain the structure and texture of the original. Sometimes it will. Sometimes it won't. If a necessary element is in the gray values, it will fail to come through, and the result can be disappointing. However, there is an excitement in the unpredictability of the end result, for there is always the possibility that some new effect will be created.

The orange-brown base color of the color negative will not cause problems in making the print. Normally, the masking color of the color negative base could be expected to act as a safelight to the ortho film. (Ortho film is insensitive to red and will reproduce it as black.) In practice this does not happen.

An image on a very grainy film was enlarged onto Kodalith to produce a line image from the natural film grain. Pushing the film increased the grain. Using Kodak 2475, a very grainy surveillance film, the model was photographed under normal room light. Ordinarily rated at ASA 1000, the film was exposed at ASA/ISO 6000, 2½ stops faster and push processed in HC 110, dilution B, for four times the usual developing time. The result is a low-contrast (because of the original very low-contrast lighting), very grainy negative. The negative was then printed on Kodalith, which emphasized the grain, providing the background tone.

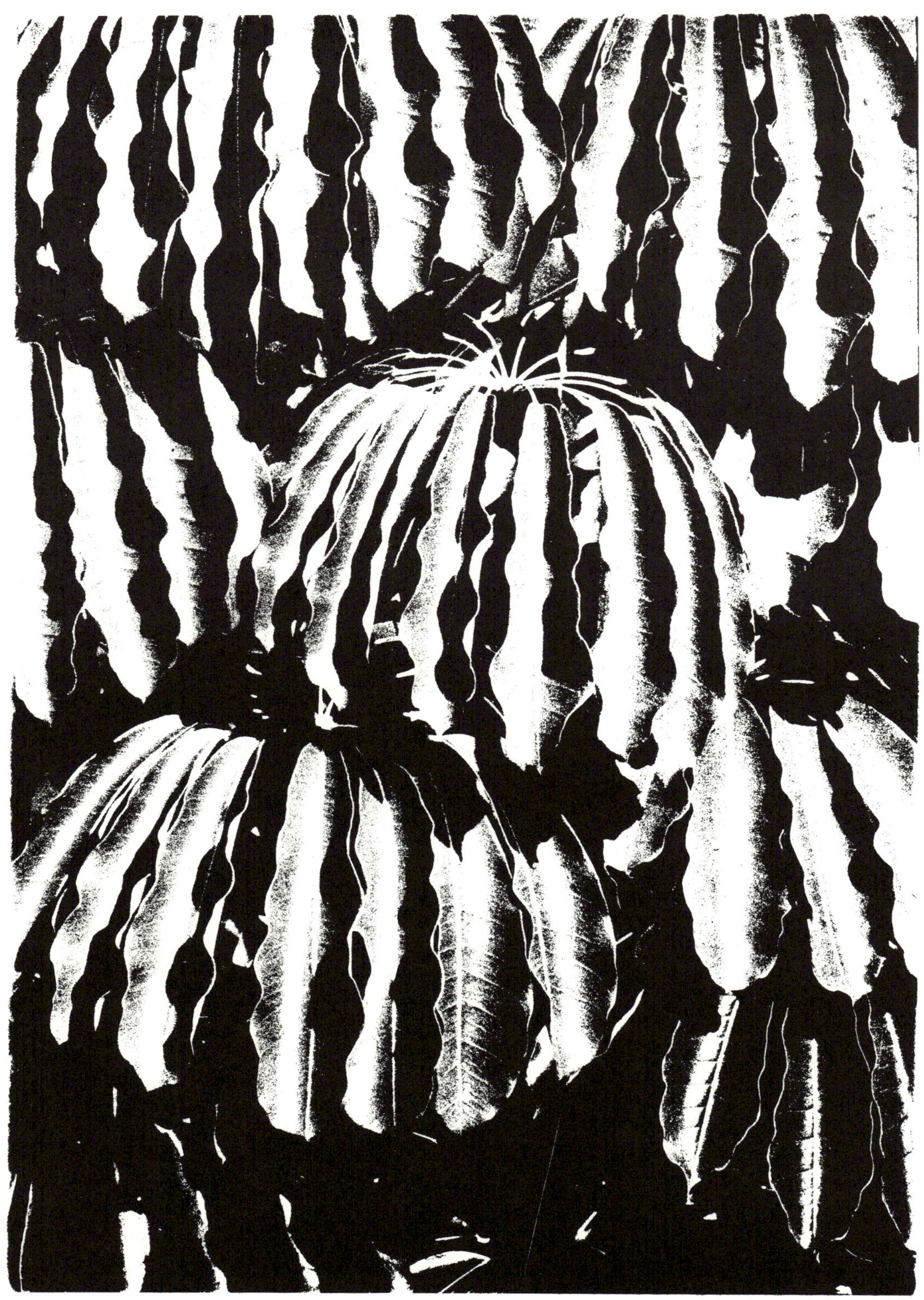

This is another negative made on Kodak 2475 film, enlarged onto Kodalith. The original negative was not pushed in development. The photograph was made on a cloudy, overcast day. Although the original negative is soft in contrast, the Kodalith exaggerates the contrast to make the leaves appear as if they were photographed in brilliant sunlight.

The versatility of Kodalith enables us to use it either in a camera or by projection under an enlarger. Try to get as much experience as possible with the new material in order to best reveal its advantages and disadvantages.

As *tone* photographers we will, almost unconsciously, follow a procedure of beginning with full-range tone images that are converted to high-contrast copies on Kodalith. This method of conversion allows a large degree of control over the image—some tones or areas can be accented, others de-emphasized. Burning-in, dodging, and bleaching with ferricyanide solution (Farmer's reducer) are all possible methods of manipulation.

However, there is a more direct path to high-contrast. Kodalith also can be used as camera film. My approach, in all new photo situations, is first to get a little technical information, then to load my camera and try it. If you have a 4″ × 5″ (10 cm × 13 cm) camera, you can load some holders with the sheet film. Otherwise, buy 35mm Kodalith in 100-foot (30.5-m) rolls, and use a bulk loader to prepare your cassettes for camera use.

As a start, try rating Kodalith at an exposure index (ASA/ISO rating) of 6. Typical exposures would be:

In bright sun:	1/125	1/30	1/4	1 sec.
	f/2.8	f/5.6	f/16	f/32
In tungsten light:	1/8	1/2	4 sec.	15 sec.
	f/2.8	f/5.6	f/16	f/32

It is advisable to take your own meter readings to ensure an exact exposure for your particular light condition. These readings given here are just average exposures to indicate the range of possibilities. An incident-light reading, or a reflected-light reading from a middle-gray card, will give the best results with average subjects.

When using Kodalith as a camera film, we do manipulation at the time of exposure. *Bracketing* exposures, shooting additional lower and higher exposures, offers one way of varying results (and of covering yourself in your first attempts to use Kodalith in this way). Suppose you are photographing a building in bright summer sunlight and the exposure reading from the meter is 1/4 sec. at f/16. Set the shutter at 1/4 sec., and bracket over and under by changing the aperture (e.g., f/11; f/16; f/22).

It seems obvious that subjects with hard edges or clearly defined outlines, such as buildings, skylines, or boat masts, will photograph well as high-contrast images. However, softer images of clouds, water, people, and clothing have turned out so well that you should feel free to experiment with them.

KODALITH AS A CAMERA FILM

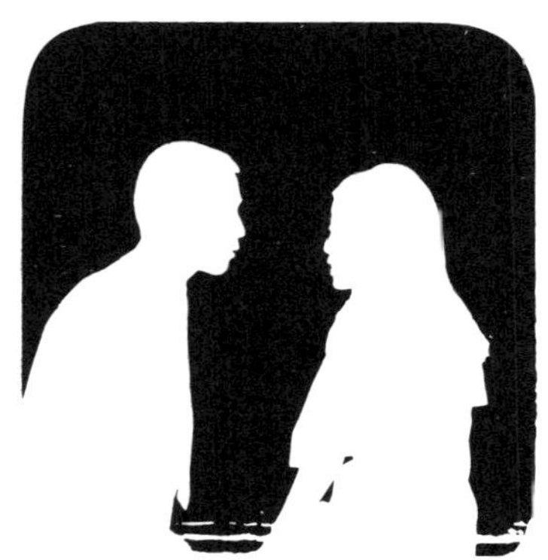

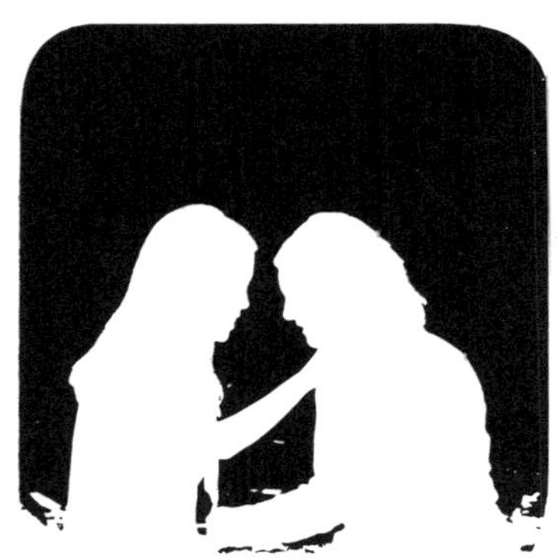

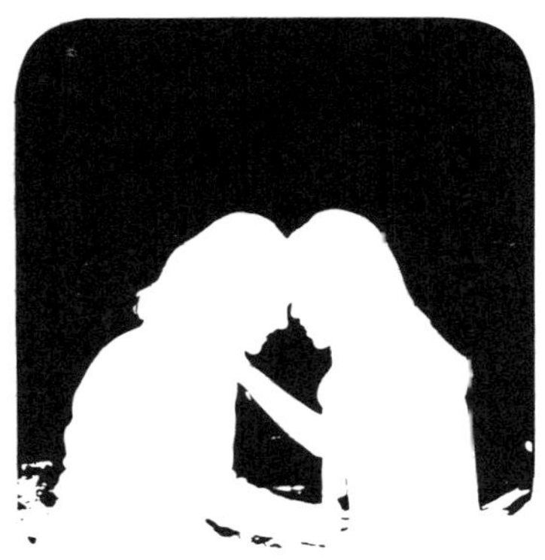

To shoot a similar picture with Kodalith in the camera, choose a subject posed against a bright background, such as the sky. Expose for the background to ensure that the subject will be well underexposed and will appear as a clear silhouette on the film.

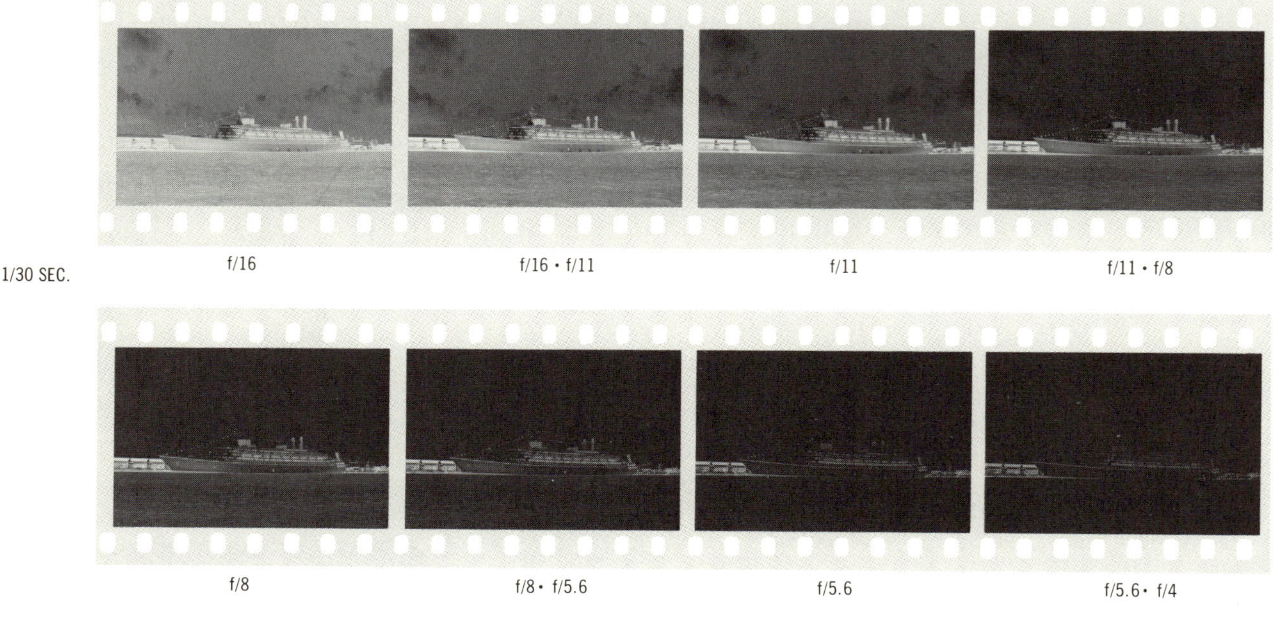

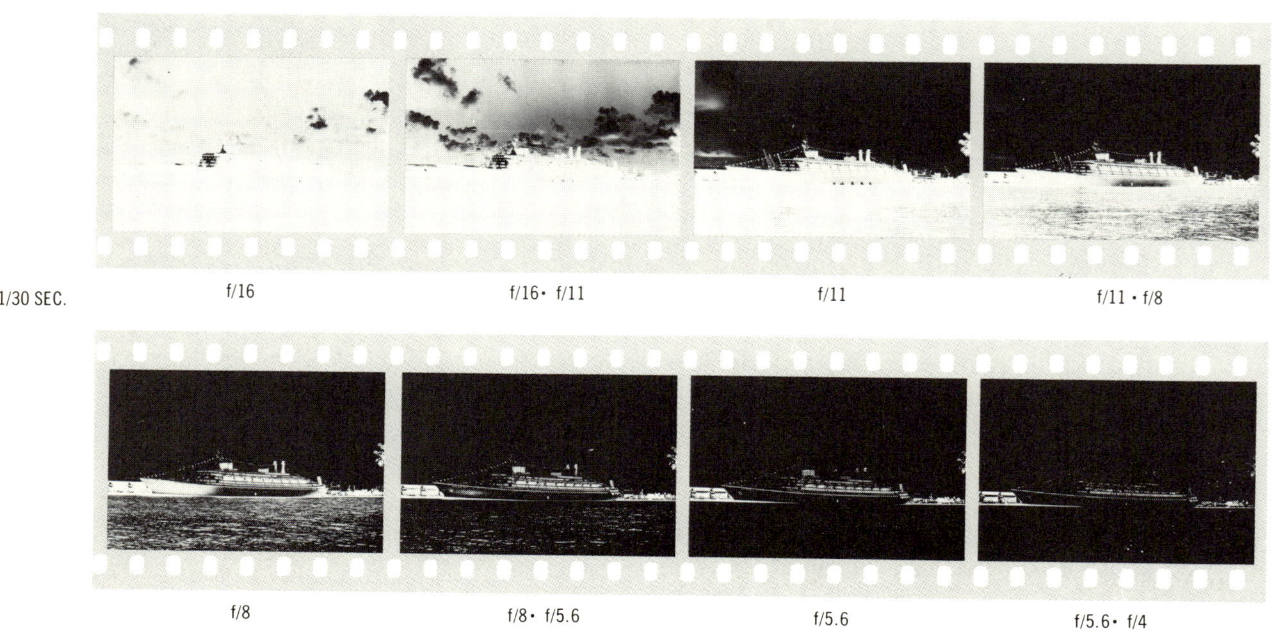

Kodalith used in the camera can produce tone, or only black and white. The top two rows show a series of exposures on Kodalith developed normally in HC 110, dilution A. The bottom two rows show matching exposures developed in Kodalith A and B developer.

Another consideration is whether a subject in bright sunlight or in the shade makes a better high-contrast photo. In my experience, subjects photographed under low-contrast conditions (in the shade, for example) exhibit more overall texture and detail.

It is possible to *push* Kodalith and get some interesting experimental results. Pushing means to rate a film at a higher than usual speed and then to compensate for the resulting reduced exposure with extended development. There is as yet no literature for pushing Kodalith, because it does not behave quite like conventional continuous-tone films. Not many photographers use this technique. You can become one of the few, but you'll have to experiment.

Kodalith can be processed in Dektol paper developer, diluted one part developer to three parts water (or even greater dilutions). It can also be processed in such film developers as D-76, HC-110, or even very fine grain developers.

Kodalith film behaves as a high-contrast material when processed in a caustic developer (Kodalith A and B). At the standard 3 min./68 F, we can predict its cut-off point. However, Kodalith can also be made to behave like a very low-contrast *tone* film by controlling the exposure and the developing time in a low-contrast film developer. Should you ever wish to prepare a black-and-white transparency with lovely nuances of tone on a clear, colorless base, try Kodalith. You won't be disappointed.

Three

Making "Negative" and "Positive" Prints with Kodalith

On the theory that subject matter is "positive," conventional photographic thinking calls a camera-film image a negative and the subsequent paper print a positive, because its light-dark balance corresponds directly to the original subject.

It is not so easy, however, to differentiate the positive from the negative. By placing an object on a sheet of print paper and causing its shadow to be recorded, we end up with a white area surrounded by black. What is negative? What is positive?

I prefer to think of the shadow as a representation of the object. Therefore I prefer the word "shadowgraph" as more descriptive of this kind of image than "photogram." If the shadow area is the representation, then logically it is the positive, whether white or black. When we simplify images to only white and black or to, perhaps, a total of three or four tones, do we get a negative or a positive? We are so far from realistic representation it is often impossible to know for sure. The real question to consider is, which is the better image?

In making *photoGRAPHICS*, try to play down realistic representation. Look at the image as a new entity without any necessary reference to "reality." Ask yourself: Is it well composed? Does it feel nicely balanced in space? It may represent the original subject, but does it look like something else? or nothing else? Does it matter? Does it feel whole? or somehow unfinished? Does it feel right to you? *You* are the final judge.

KODALITH CONTACT PRINTS

Supplies and equipment

Kodalith Ortho Sheet film, 4″ × 5″ (10 cm × 13 cm)

Kodalith developer, A and B

Stop bath

Fixer (acid hardening)

Hypo clearing agent

Safelight, 1A light red

Plate glass, apparently 5″ × 7″ (13 cm × 18 cm)

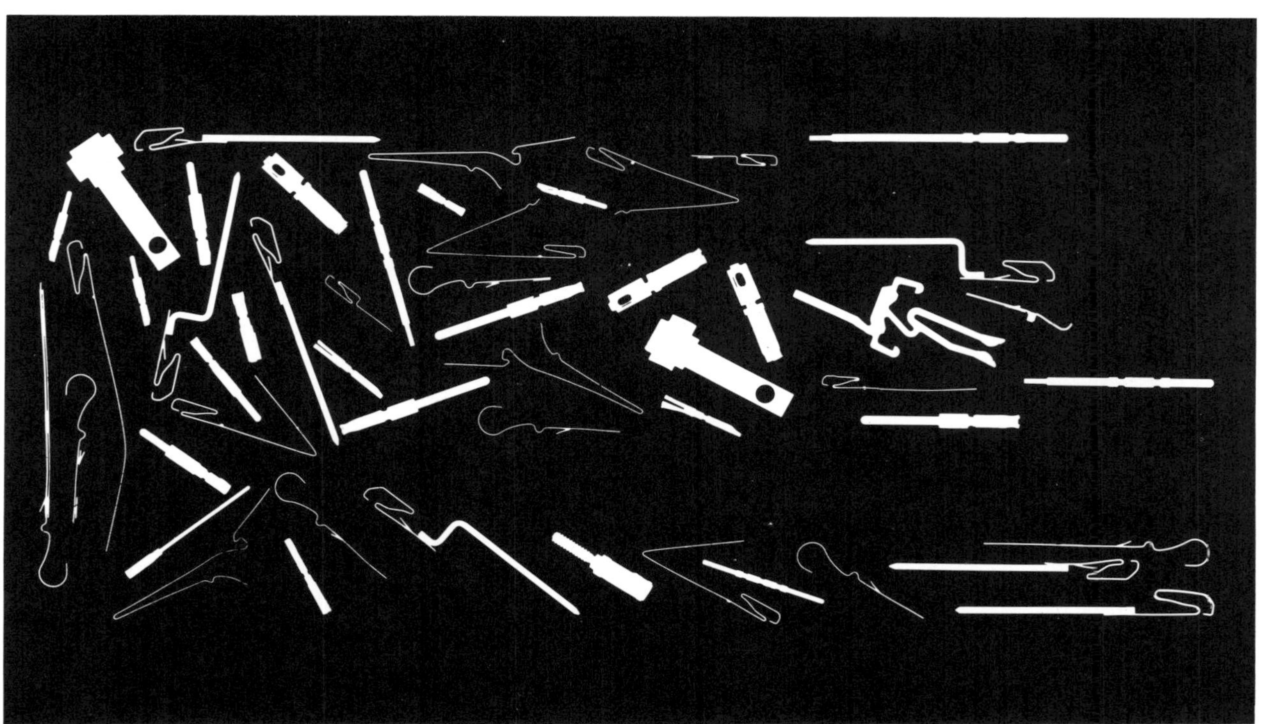

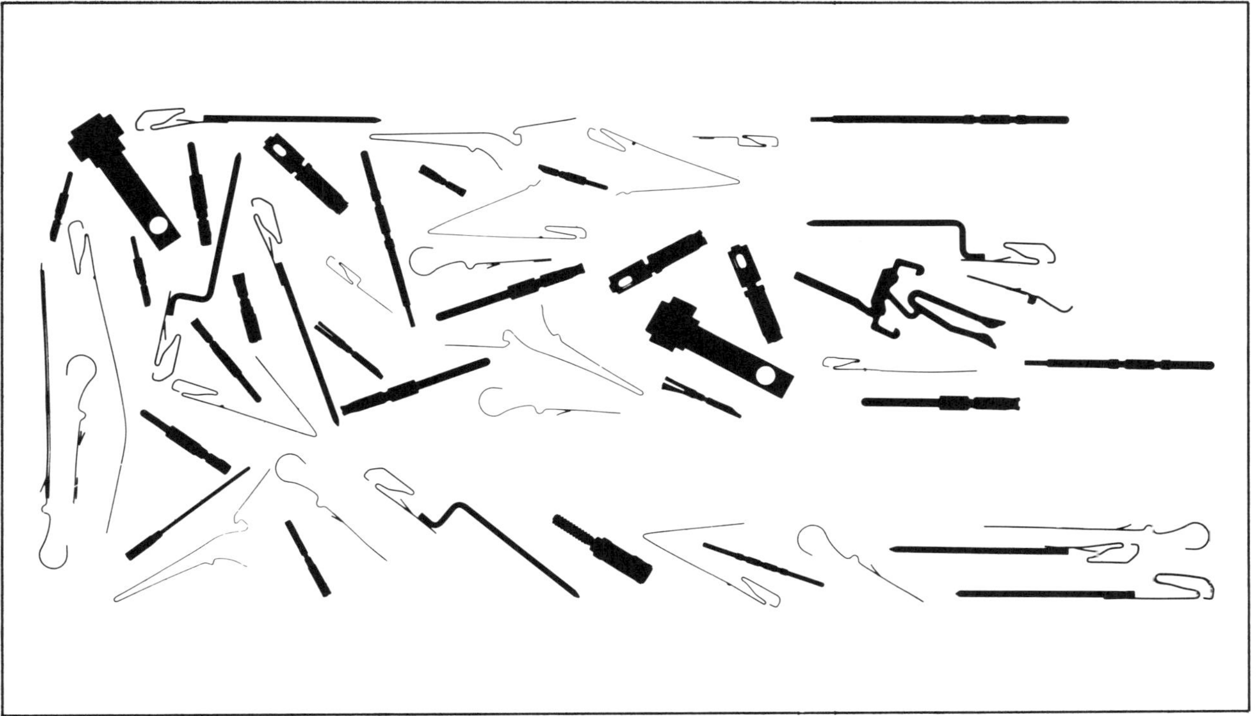

These electronic parts were placed on a light table and photographed
directly on Kodalith, which produced black areas on clear film. A contact
print made from that image produced white areas on a black
background—the version used for this impressive advertising illustration.

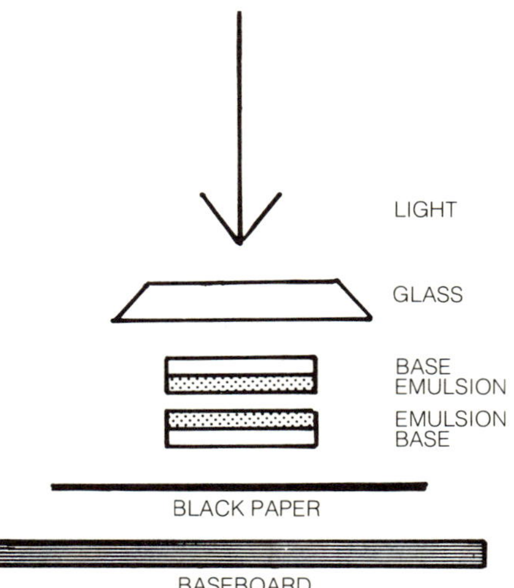

To contact print films, place them emulsion to emulsion, with a piece of black paper underneath to prevent reflected exposure. A glass plate on top will ensure complete contact between the emulsions.

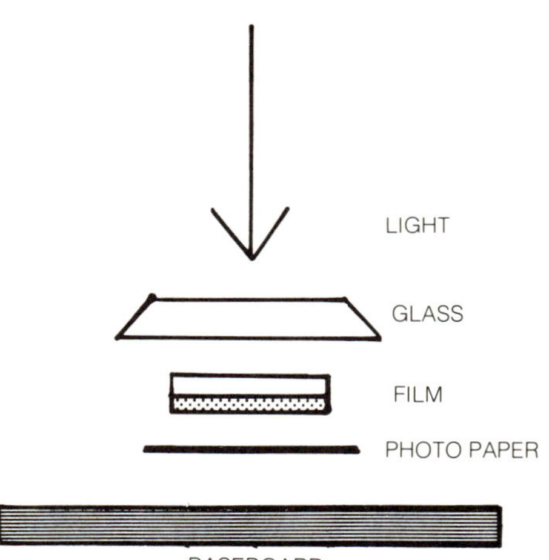

Contact printing Kodalith onto paper is no different from ordinary contact printing procedures. The paper is emulsion side up, the film emulsion side down. No black backing paper is required, because the print base is opaque.

Procedure: Kodalith on Kodalith

Just as you would contact print a film image onto paper, so you will now print film to film — emulsion to emulsion (dull side), weighting them down with the plate glass to ensure complete contact between emulsions. To prevent halation put black paper on the baseboard under the glass and films. The enlarger will again become your light source. Expose the packet of film, then process the film print in Kodalith A and B developer. It is wise to make a test strip of your first try. When you have determined the proper exposure from the test strip, proceed to the final print.

You will now have two pieces of film in your hands made by contact printing one piece of film to the other. One is negative, the other is positive. But which is which? If you started this procedure with a black-and-white or a color negative in the enlarger, the first Kodalith film would be positive. However, if the starting point was a color slide (positive), the first Kodalith would be negative. This set of negative and positive films will be used for the next step and will then be taken further in Chapter 5, which covers line-drawing prints.

Procedure: Kodalith film to paper

Contact print the Kodalith film to photo paper in the usual manner. The paper should be emulsion side up, the film emulsion side down. No black backing paper is required, because the print base is opaque. If you are using the enlarger as a light source, you will need enlarging paper. Should you prefer a contact printer, use contact paper. Its slower speed is adjusted for the brighter light emitted by this type of equipment. Photo paper has contrast grades ranging from "0" (soft) to "5" (contrasty). Kodalith, because of its extreme contrast, will print well on *any* grade.

Study the image you have produced. If you like the effect, place one or the other of the films in the enlarger, and blow it up to a size appropriate for viewing or exhibition. Push pin your prints to the wall and look at them from time to time. If you tire of an image, put it away. Those still hanging after three months are definitely winners.

Try mounting your Kodaliths over colored papers. Gold, silver, mirror-finished mylar, or any of the fluorescent colors are especially recommended. Hang these, too, to see the effect. Your judgment is totally valid, but it takes time to get over the first flush of creativity. Some photographers cherish even their test strips, because they made them. As you gain more experience, you will learn to separate the good prints from the bad.

The illustration on page 41 shows Kodalith printing variations. Kodalith film, contact printed to Kodalith film,

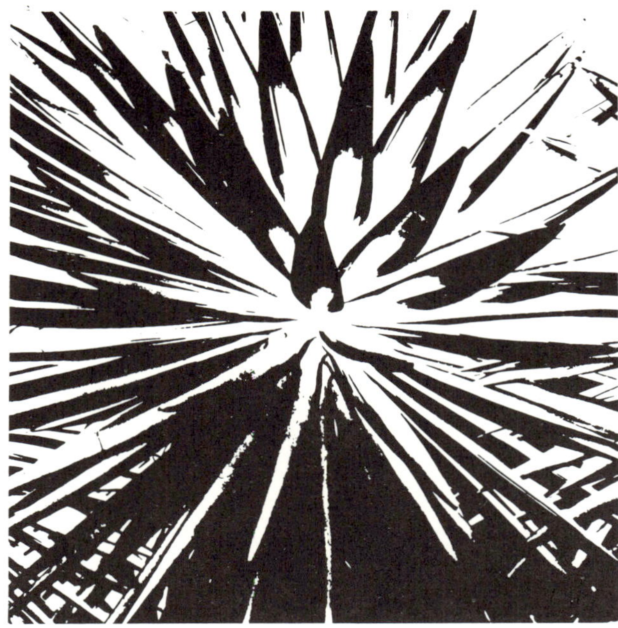

A. *A negative image on Kodalith.*

B. *A positive image on Kodalith, contact printed from (A).*

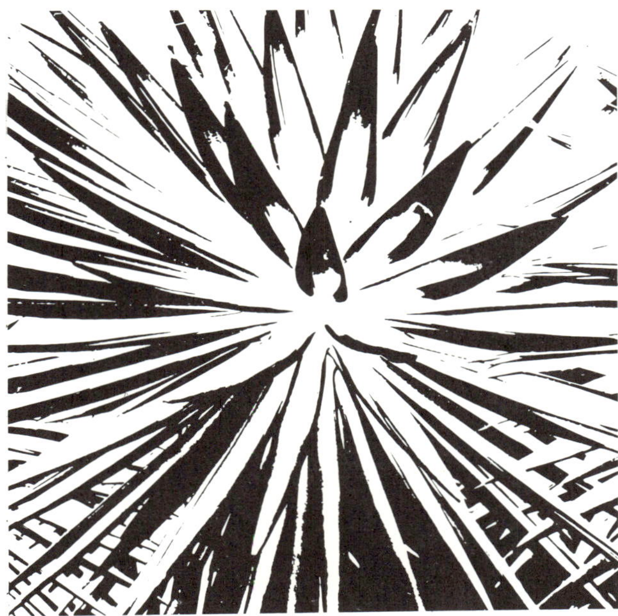

A positive print on paper, made from (A).

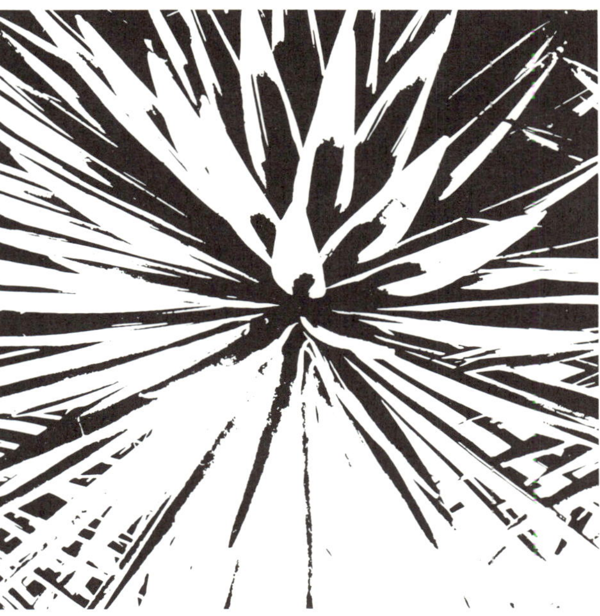

A negative print on paper, made from (B).

will create a negative and a positive of the same subject. The films are placed emulsion to emulsion and then backed by a sheet of black matte paper. The negative faces the light source. The next step is to print the negative and the positive onto photo paper, either by contact or by enlarging.

Four

Registering Kodaliths

In the processes of masking and posterization, two or more films are placed together and printed as one single exposure. It is necessary to asssemble the multiple negatives so accurately that when the print is viewed they will align so you cannot see any double lines or image irregularities. This is called exact *registration*.

When *masking*, we effect a change in the original image by reducing or increasing highlights, or by blocking unwanted areas. In *posterization*, we print selected density segments, one after another, on the same sheet of paper. Registration may be done visually, by placing the negatives on a light table, sliding them past each other until they align perfectly, and then taping them together. But this is not easy to do, nor is it precise.

The following mechanical method is a simplification of the professional methods used in graphic arts plants. Accuracy is achieved by punching matching sets of holes in the films before exposure. Done carefully, the films will register to each other by centering on pins. In graphic arts plants, special punches and stainless steel strips manufactured for the purpose of registration are used. But at this stage in our development as photographers, it isn't necessary to purchase specialized or sophisticated equipment.

You can punch holes with an inexpensive two- or three-hole stationery punch and a pin register board can be made with wood dowels or metal pins. (The wood dowels can be bought at a hardware store or lumber yard; the metal pins are available from graphic arts supply houses.) Use Bregman pins or the equivalent. Attach them with some masking tape to a sheet of plywood painted black, or a piece of matte black cardboard that will fit into your paper easel.

REGISTRATION **Supplies and equipment**

> Same as for exposing Kodalith film
>
> Plate glass
>
> Hole punch
>
> Pin register board

As an exercise in registration, select a new subject, and repeat the previous exercise in preparation of a Kodalith film. This time, hole punch the film, center it on the pins,

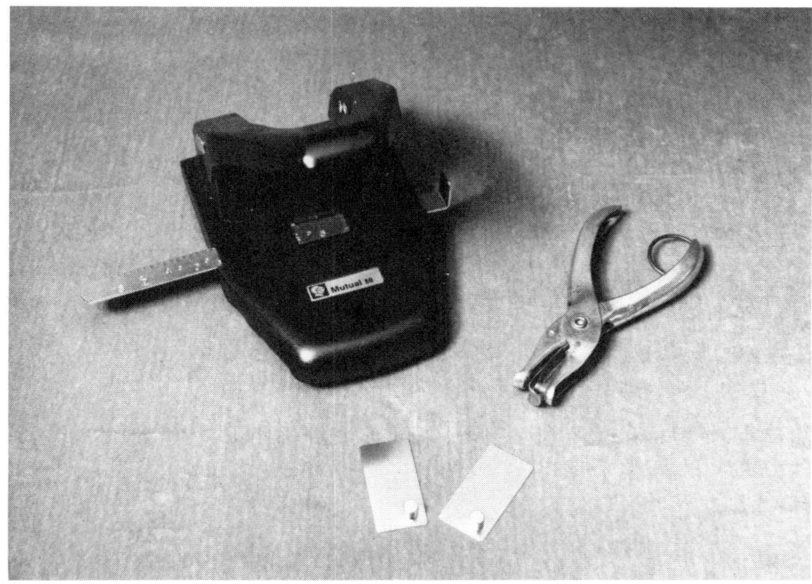

An ordinary two- or three-hole stationery punch can be used to register-punch films. Set the guide bar so that the holes in the film are centered, then tape the film securely in position. A hand punch can be used to edge notch the sheets of a registered set for identification. Register pins (bottom center) can be attached to any convenient surface.

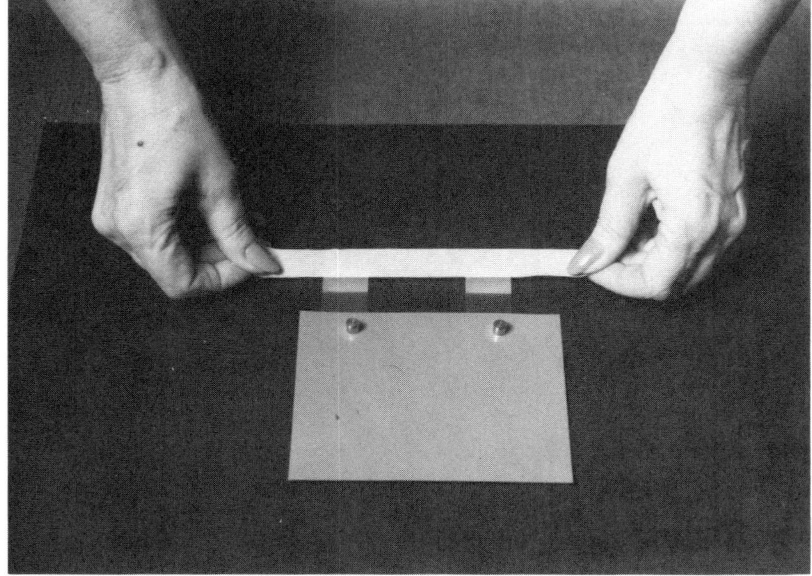

To locate the pins accurately, slip them into the holes of a prepunched sheet of scrap film or cardboard, then tape the pins in position. In this photo, the pins have been fastened onto a piece of matte black board that fits a large-size printing frame.

weight it with plate glass, and then expose.

Hopefully, you made a careful record of the previous exposure, so that you could repeat the same time and aperture setting. If not, run a new test strip to determine the proper time and opening.

Instructions

Step 1. *Expose the Kodalith*
Expose; process; wash; dry.

Step 2. *Contact print*
Contact print the Kodalith film to an unexposed Kodalith film.

Punch holes in the new film, and then place it on the pin register board emulsion (dull) side *up.* Cover it with the first film, emulsion side *down.* Cover with the plate glass and expose.

Step 3. *Expose the contact printed Kodalith*

Expose; process; wash; dry. Record the column height, aperture opening, and time in seconds for this exposure, so you can repeat it and be fairly confident that the exposure will be correct. Remember that if, in the interim, you change the column height or other variables, you will have to rerun a test for the correct exposure.

When contact printing on Kodalith, there are two things that can go wrong. One is lack of intimate contact, the other is under or overexposure. If there is too little exposure, the black areas will appear thin with pinholes throughout; if there is too much, the black will become extra dense and will expand into the clear area. The correct exposure is a solid black with a sharp edge.

Right. *These three films, each two-hole punched, will register to each other. They can be assembled on a set of pins, exposed, removed, reassembled, and the images will line up (register) perfectly each time.*

Opposite page. *"Gull in Flight," a tone-simplified image, required three negatives: dark background, white gull, and single gray tone, which gives a sense of volume to the body and wings. Use of the hole-punch system described in this chapter ensured that the films would print in perfect register. The technique of tone simplification, or* posterization, *is described in Chapters 7 and 8.*

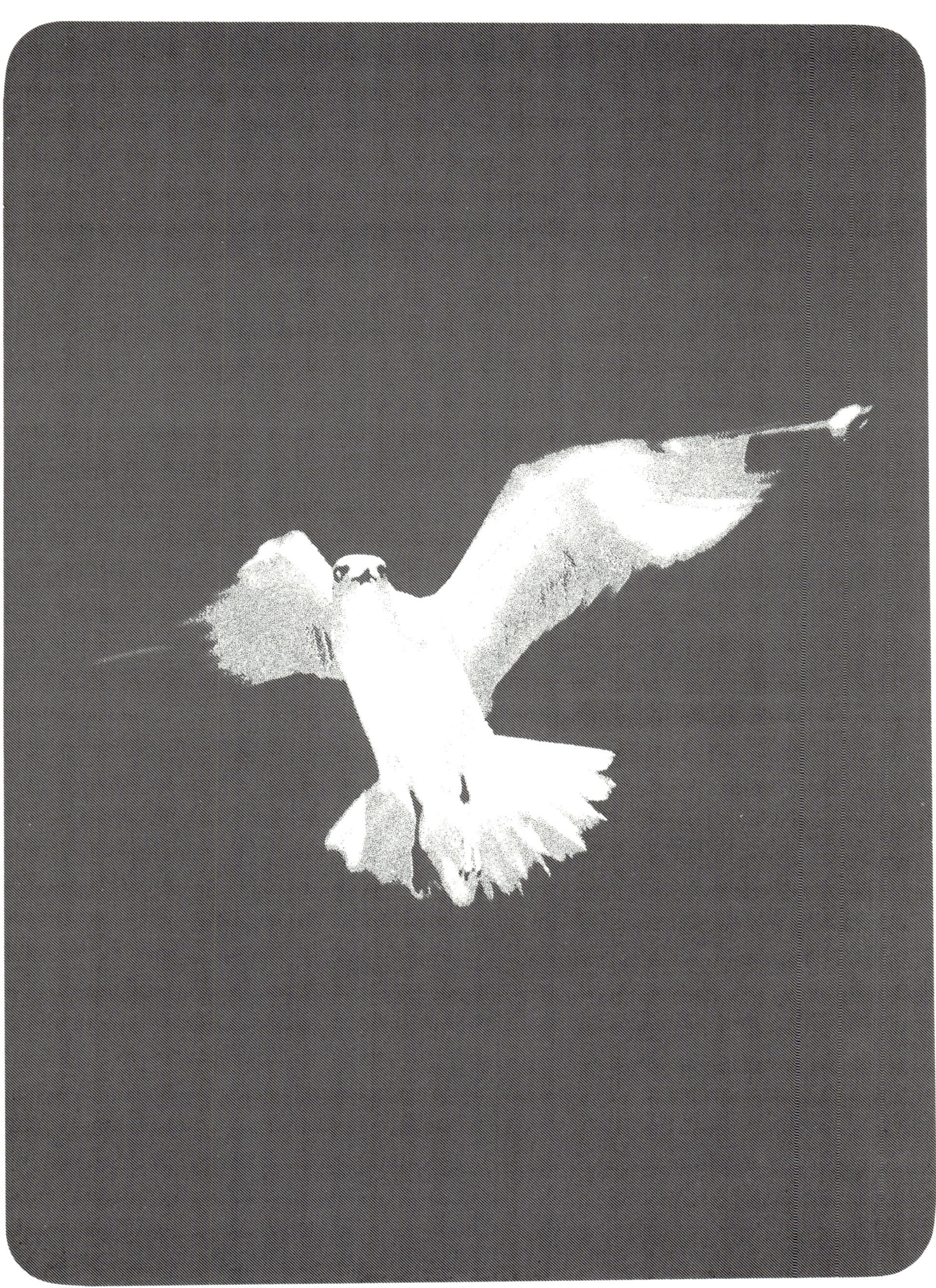

Five

How to Create a Line-Drawing Print with Kodalith

You now have two register-punched sheets of film with matching images of opposite tonality. When the film image was produced by contact, the two emulsions were face to face. By exposure, we produced a perfect opposite. Consider one image a negative, the other a positive. Another way to look at them is to value one at 50 percent and the other at 50 percent. Together they make 100 percent of the image.

If we place one image over the other in perfect register, they will cancel each other, and we will see neither light nor an image. If we try to pass the light directly through the set of films, we will not be able to do so. Opposite areas in high-contrast negatives and positives are opaque. When they are registered emulsion to emulsion, light from all angles is blocked.

If we separate the two films slightly and create a clear space between them, we will be able to slip light through, but only at a 45-degree angle. If we place this sandwich on a piece of film or paper and expose through it that way, the result will be a thin line of exposure around each image area—a *line-drawing print*, so named because it looks like a pen and ink drawing.

A line-drawing print is an interesting derivation. Theoretically, it should work with any image. In fact, it is most effective when the image is composed largely of lines or hard edges. Buildings and trees are especially good subjects.

LINE-DRAWING PRINT

Supplies and equipment

> 25-watt white or clear bulb
>
> Cord and socket for this bulb
>
> Kodalith film, or enlarging paper
>
> Processing chemicals for the film or paper

Instructions

Place the two films back-to-back and register the images. They will be separated by two thicknesses of clear film base.

Prepare to expose with light at a 45-degree angle. This

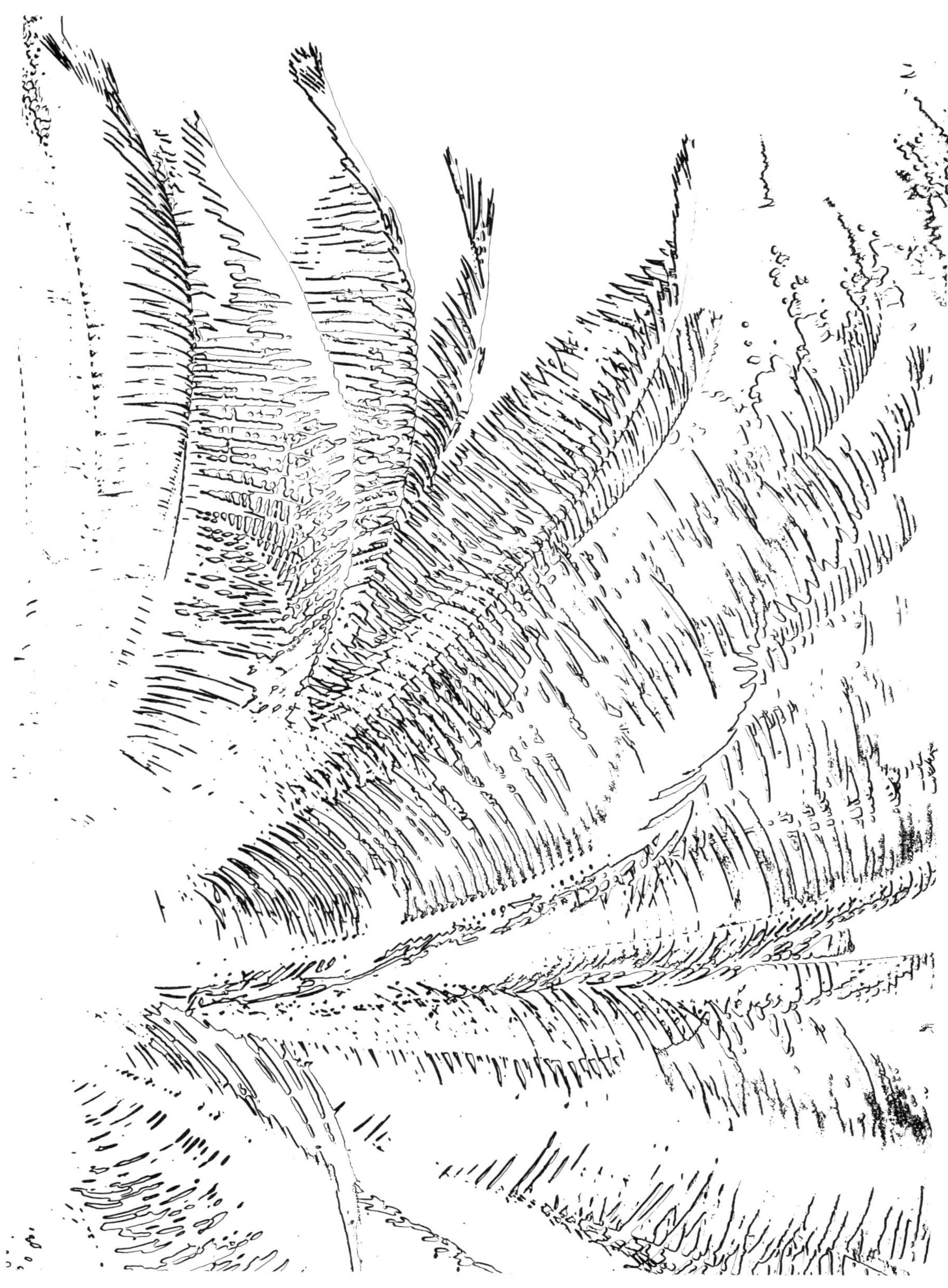

"Palm Fronds," a line-drawing print photoGRAPHICALLY created. Line drawing produces a delicate effect of tracery. It can be combined with other techniques, such as posterization, but it is essential to maintain accurate registration throughout.

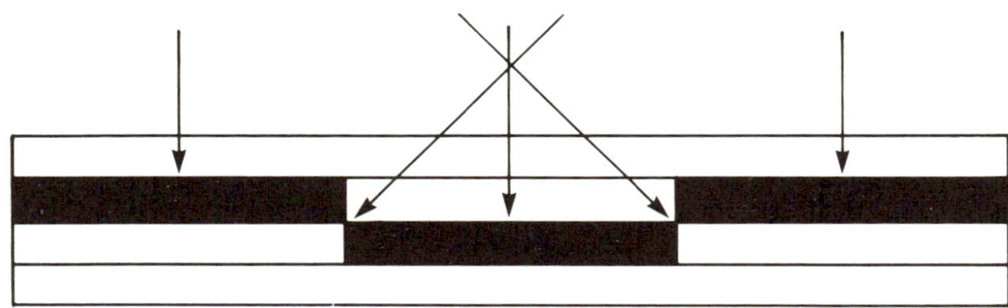

Opposite areas in high-contrast negatives and positives are opaque. When they are registered emulsion to emulsion, light from all angles is blocked.

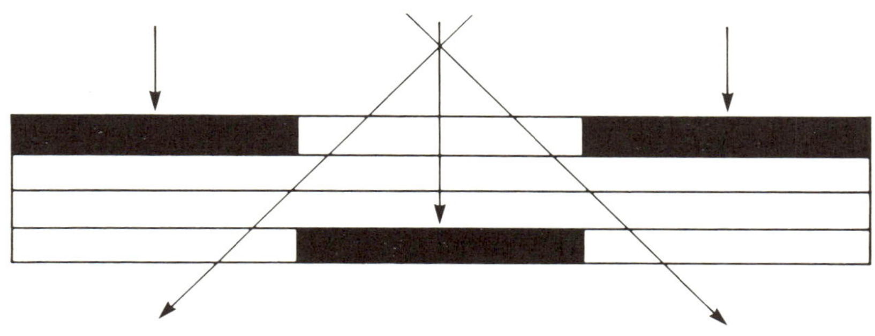

When registered base to base, there is just enough separation of the images to permit angled light to pass but head-on light is blocked. As a result, a thin line of light along the edge of each image area can expose an emulsion placed below this sandwich. For the sake of clarity, the space is exaggerated here.

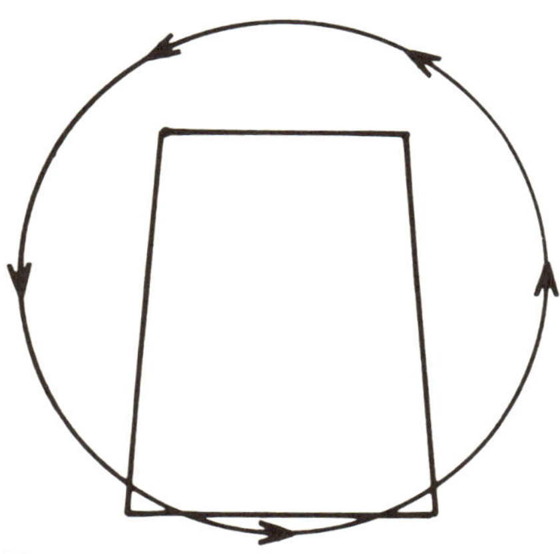

To ensure complete line-drawing exposure, the angled light must strike the films from every direction. It may be easier to move the light in a circular path than to revolve the printing setup.

will create a small mechanical problem, because the light must be rotated a full 360 degrees around the films, at a 45-degree angle from their surface.

You can use a print frame on a turntable, mounting the light in a fixed position above. A phonograph turntable revolved by hand will also work, as would a lazy Susan, a kitchen storage accessory. I find it much easier to hold the light in my hand and rotate it around the printing setup continuously during the exposure. Try it; it's simple and works well. Use a timer, or count seconds to yourself. The light should pass entirely around the films several times during the exposure.

The exposure may be made on Kodalith film or on photo paper. The choice is based on your chosen route to the final print.

Option 1.   Kodalith film

Kodalith is the ideal choice for this work. When properly exposed and developed, the film image will appear as a number of very fine lines.

The final print can be made by contact or enlargement from this film. Or you can reverse the image by contact printing this Kodalith onto another sheet of Kodalith, as we explained in Chapter 3. Compare the two images. Do

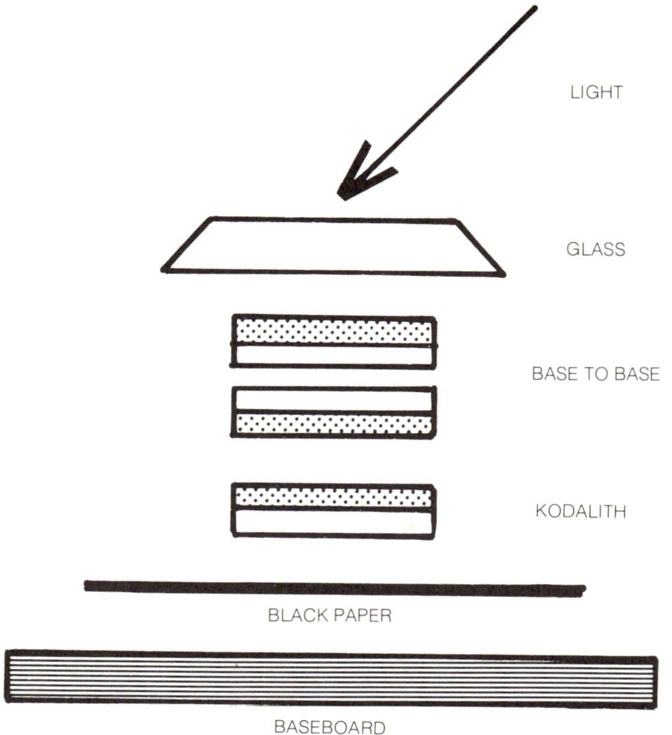

Setup for printing line drawings: base-to-base negative and positive images are placed above the emulsion-side-up Kodalith film to be exposed. As in all film-to-film printing, black backing paper and a glass pressure plate are required.

you prefer black lines on white, or white lines on black? Note the extent of possible variations. (Throughout this book suggestions of new ideas and variations are intended to open avenues for your own experimentation.)

Option 2. *Paper print*

The final print may be made directly from the registered sandwich onto paper. The choice of contact or enlarging paper will be determined by the intensity of the exposing light.

For experimenting, testing, and gaining experience with these new materials, it's wise to work with small sizes. This will help to keep the cost down, too. When you have gained assurance and expertise, it will be time to consider working with 11″ × 14″ (28 cm × 36 cm) or even 16″ × 20″ (41 cm × 51 cm) Kodalith.

The final line-drawing print should have a light, airy, sketchy look about it. If you think the lines are too thin, they can be thickened or strengthened by increasing the clear space between the two films. The spacing is accomplished by placing a sheet or two of clear acetate between the films. Any clear sheet plastic material of 0.005- or 0.0075-inch (0.13 or 0.19-mm) thickness is suitable and is readily available at art supply stores.

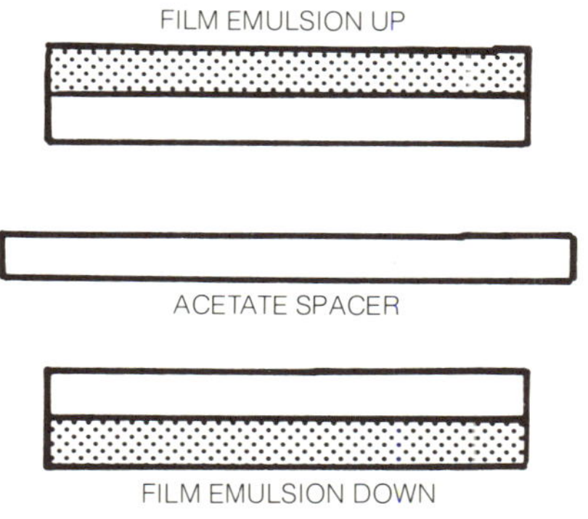

To produce thicker lines in your photoGRAPHIC drawings, increase the negative–positive separation with a clear plastic or acetate spacer.

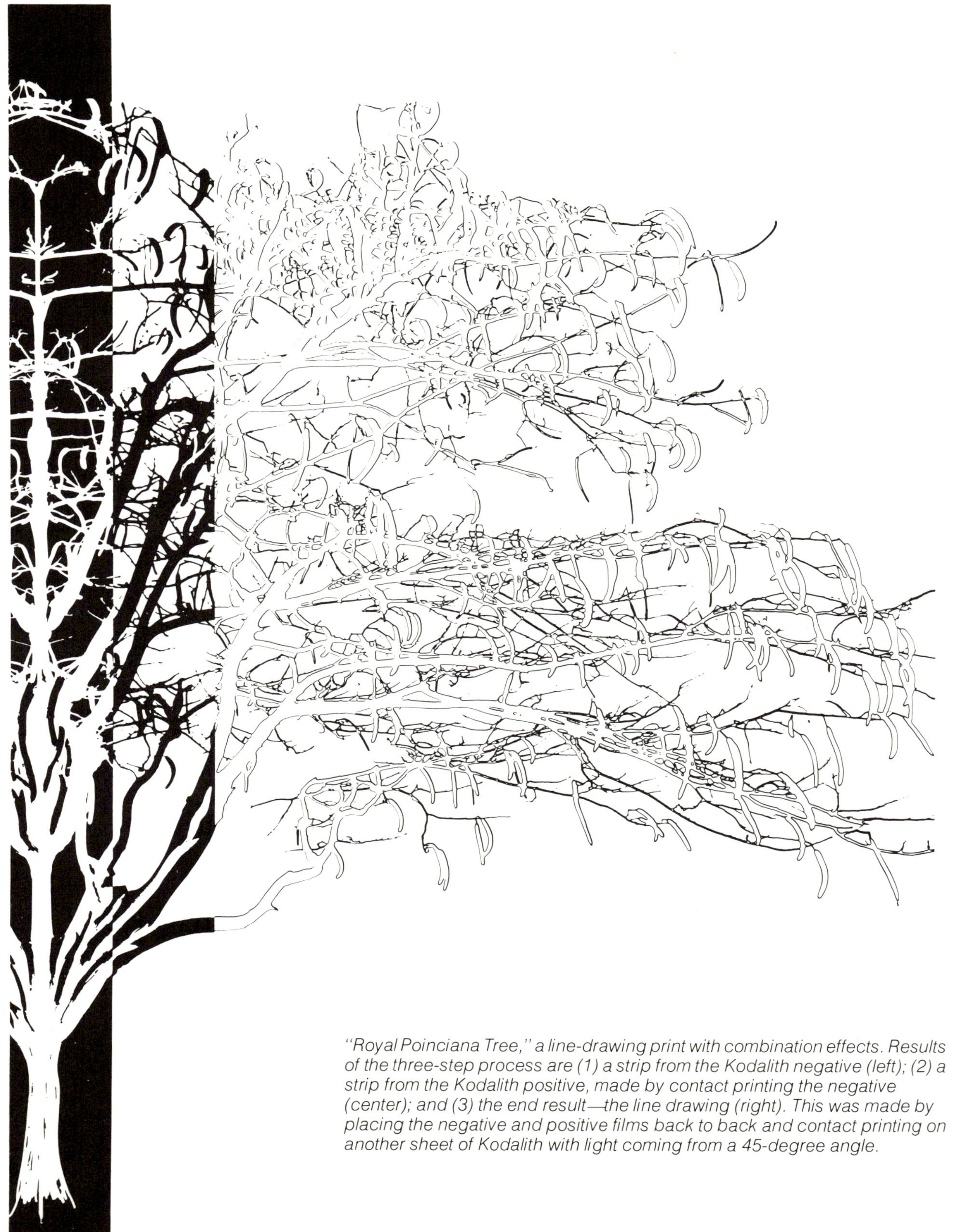

"Royal Poinciana Tree," a line-drawing print with combination effects. Results of the three-step process are (1) a strip from the Kodalith negative (left); (2) a strip from the Kodalith positive, made by contact printing the negative (center); and (3) the end result—the line drawing (right). This was made by placing the negative and positive films back to back and contact printing on another sheet of Kodalith with light coming from a 45-degree angle.

Tone Separation or Density Slicing

This is the high point of *photoGRAPHIC* techniques. Mastering the tone separation and reconstruction procedures explained here will give you the key to almost infinite image variations. The plan is to take an image and "slice" it into four portions—four tone, or density levels. Each slice or segment will contain parts of the entire image, and each will be of a single density.

At this point, keep in mind that the gray scale pictured in this book is for *continuous-tone* photographs. Looking at a photograph and sorting out all the white, light-gray, or dark-gray areas accurately calls for some skill and experience. For easier understanding, we are using a straightforward scale, which corresponds to the tones in an original photograph but in an ordered sequence.

In this chapter, we will learn how to *slice*, or simplify, the full tonal range into four sections: white, light gray, dark gray, and black. Every tone in the image (or the gray scale) will be converted to one of these four values. The word slice aptly describes this action.

Kodalith film, processed in Kodalith A and B developer, is ideal for making these photographic slices because of its sharp cut-off point. That is, it changes abruptly from no density (clear) to maximum density (black). The opposed gray scale, shown here, illustrates this: it breaks down a full-range continuous-tone image (represented by the scale) into two tonal halves. Actually, there are two scales, aligned oppositely so the "break" or cut-off point can be clearly determined.

It will be helpful to visualize the process as a whole before performing the steps by studying the following explanation with its accompanying diagrams: Think of the gray scale as an image on film. If it is a positive image, the thinnest densities represent white and the lightest grays.

A gray scale is a convenient way to sort out the tones in a black-and-white continuous-tone photograph for visualization and testing.

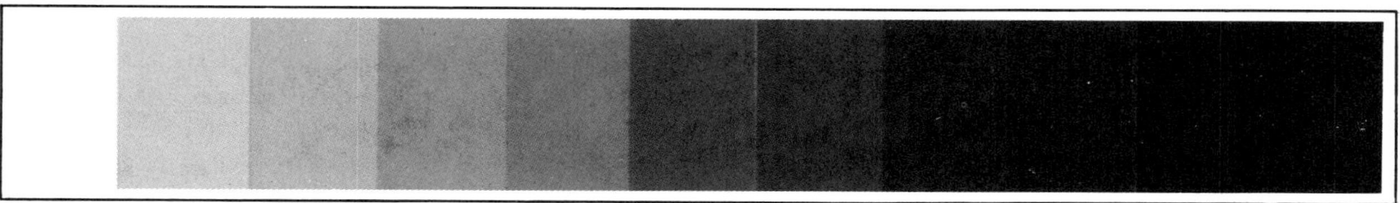

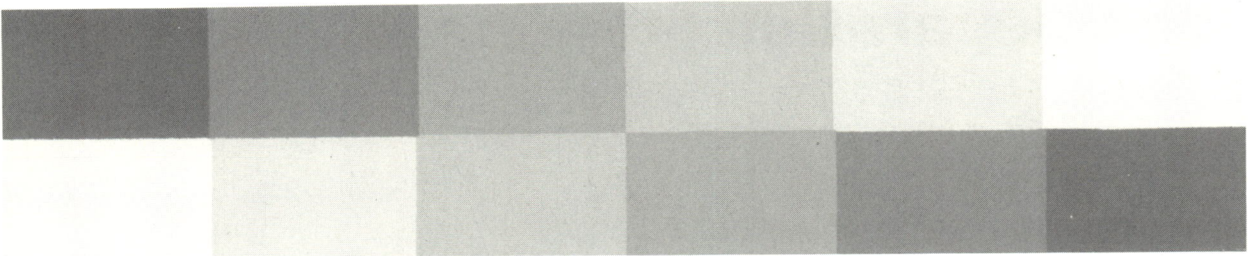

An opposed gray scale makes it easy to test the effect of various exposures on Kodalith. You can either buy one, or paste one up from two scales. The scale can be *photographed directly with Kodalith in the camera. Or, you can make a continuous-tone negative of the scale to print onto Kodalith by contact or projection (enlargement).*

The opaque portions in a test from an opposed gray scale show the break point—*the step at which exposure does affect the test emulsion. Here, a mid-scale break is shown.* *Less exposure would produce shorter opaque bars; more exposure would produce longer, overlapping bars.*

If it is a negative image, they represent the darkest tones of the original subject. For the purpose of clarity, we will assume the scale is a positive image and that the thin densities are, therefore, light tones.

In a gray scale divided into four sections, the first two steps fall in the range that will appear white in a conversion. Expose through the gray scale onto a sheet of Kodalith just enough to print through these two steps; everything else is too dense to let light through. The processed film will be black in the first two-step portion and clear everywhere else. This becomes a printing mask to block light in that portion — it is slice I, the white mask.

This film and all succeeding sheets must be hole punched, so they can be exposed in register. First register the white mask on top of another sheet of Kodalith. Then increase exposure just enough to print through the next two density steps on the gray scale, the light-gray slice.

The white mask prevents exposure in the portion it covers, the heavier densities in the gray-scale image prevent exposure in their areas. But only the two light-gray steps will affect the second sheet of film. When processed, only that portion will be black. This is slice II, the light-gray mask.

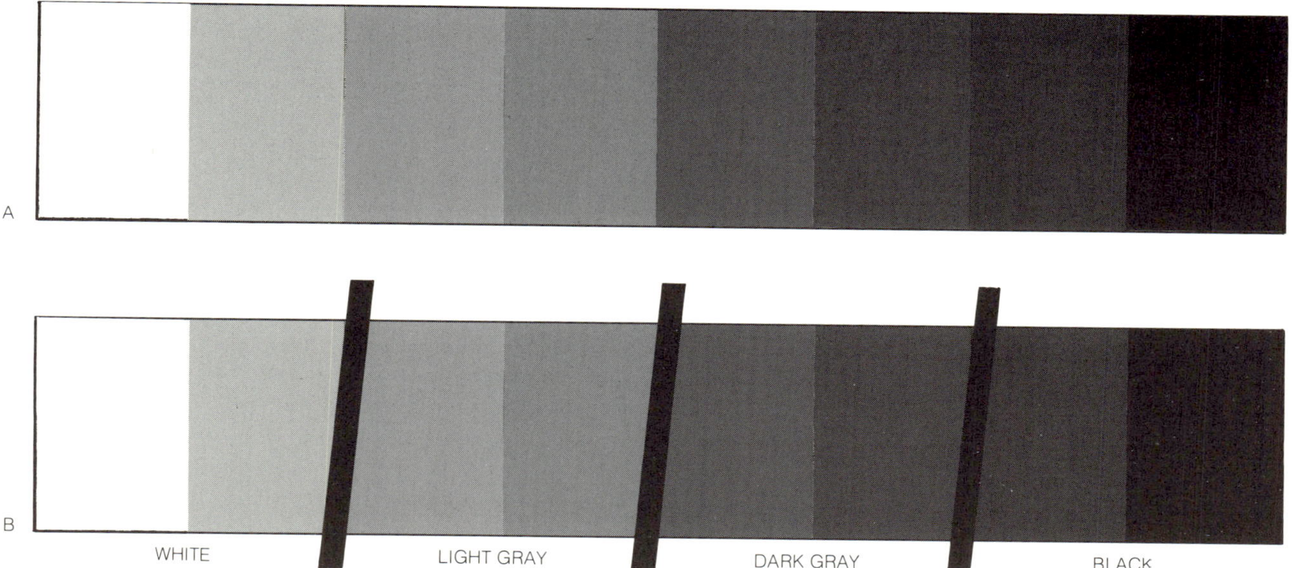

In tone separation, or density slicing, we (A) simplify a gray scale, the continuous-tone range of a photograph, into (B) a smaller number of steps. In this example, two steps are simplified into a single separation.

To make slice III, the dark-gray mask, register the two completed masks on top of a third sheet of Kodalith. Expose just enough to print through the dark-gray tones. The masks protect the lighter-tone areas; the image densities protect the darkest areas. Only the two dark-gray steps will print on slice III.

To make slice IV, the black-area mask, remove the gray scale. You can't print through its maximum-density step, and you don't need it. If you put masks I, II, and III together, the clear portions they have in common will correspond to the last two steps of the gray scale. Stack them in register on a fourth sheet of film. Expose it. When processed, it will be black only in the darkest-step areas; everything else will be blocked by the masks.

CAREFUL! To avoid mistakes, think about the exposure sequence before you actually begin.

You can determine the mask I exposure by a series of test steps. It must be just enough to print through the greatest density of that tone slice — the second step of the gray scale in our example. The exposure for mask II obviously has to be greater, because it has to get through heavier densities. And the exposure for mask III has to be even more.

But for mask IV, you do not use the gray scale. Remember, you are printing only through the clear areas of the other three masks. Your exposure, therefore, will be *less*, not more. It will be equal to or less than the mask I exposure. You may have to test to get an accurate reading.

Why not just blast plenty of light through the three masks to make mask IV? If you do, overexposure will produce thick, fuzzy edges around the image areas. The registration will be imprecise, and the outlines of objects will be blurred.

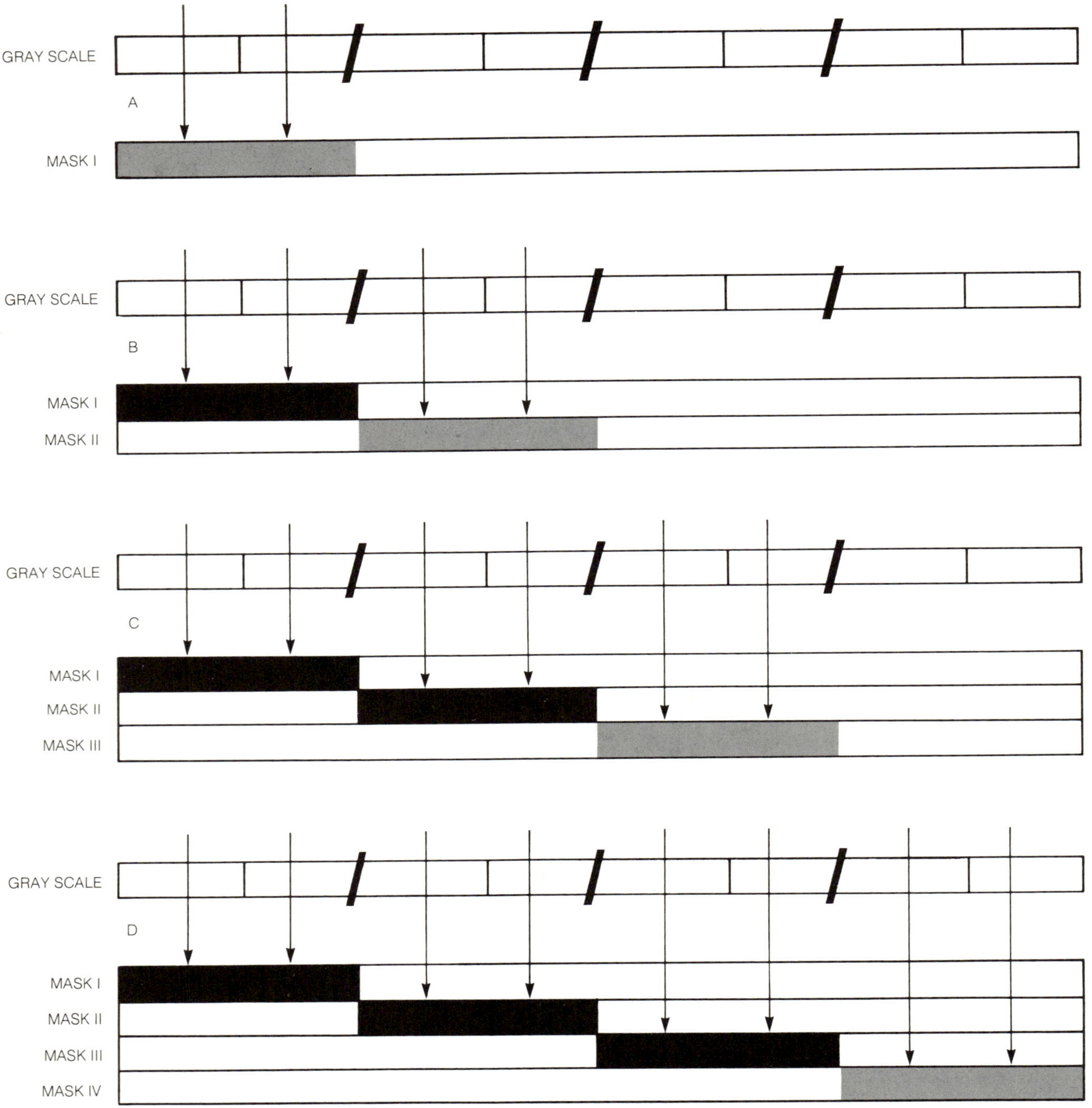

In these diagrams illustrating the process of making tone-separation masks, the top layer represents a gray scale divided into four sections, as shown at the beginning of the chapter.

A. The exposure for mask I is only enough to print through the first two steps of the scale.

B. Mask I is used to block exposure in the first two steps during the increased exposure required to make mask II.

C. Both masks I and II are required when the exposure is made for mask III.

D. The first three masks must be combined for the mask IV exposure. As explained in the text, it is not necessary to print through the gray scale (or image negative) to make the mask for the solid black step.

Underexposure creates a different problem: the black will appear thin and weak and may not be dense enough to block exposures for heavier densities.

Check these things as you go along. If something is wrong with any mask, it can be remade, providing you register everything on the pins each time. During the process of making each mask, check its registration (after processing) against the others on a light table. If properly made, the image areas will fit together perfectly; there will be no overlaps.

Once again, think of a continuous-tone image, rather than the gray scale, as your exposure source. The slice I exposure will produce masking densities on the Kodalith wherever the image is very thin. The same will be true for masks II, III, and IV. They will be opaque wherever their corresponding densities occur in the image; all other areas will be clear.

You can print masks from a camera negative, a positive conversion, a color transparency or negative, or any image on film. They can be made with an enlarger, or by contact printing—if the original is big enough to be register punched. (If not, tape a scrap sheet of film to the original to provide sufficient margin for hole punching.) For your first trials, use a camera film negative in black and white.

Important point: Under ordinary circumstances, we would place a negative in the enlarger with the emulsion toward the lens (or in a contact printer with the emulsion toward the material exposed) and the base side facing the light source. However, when making photographic slices, the negative must be *turned over*, emulsion (dull) side toward the light source. By reversing the image at this stage, it will read correctly when we make a final print. In other words, right will be on the right, left on the left. If your final print is "wrong reading," the probable cause is failure to reverse the negative.

In conventional tone printing, we place the negative and print paper in an emulsion-to-emulsion position. The emulsion side of the final paper print will, therefore, have the correct reading image. However, when we wish to produce an intermediate film, which will in turn be used to print on paper or film, it is necessary to have a flopped image, or reverse reading, on the emulsion side. Then, when the intermediate film is turned over to be conventionally printed, the new print will be "right reading."

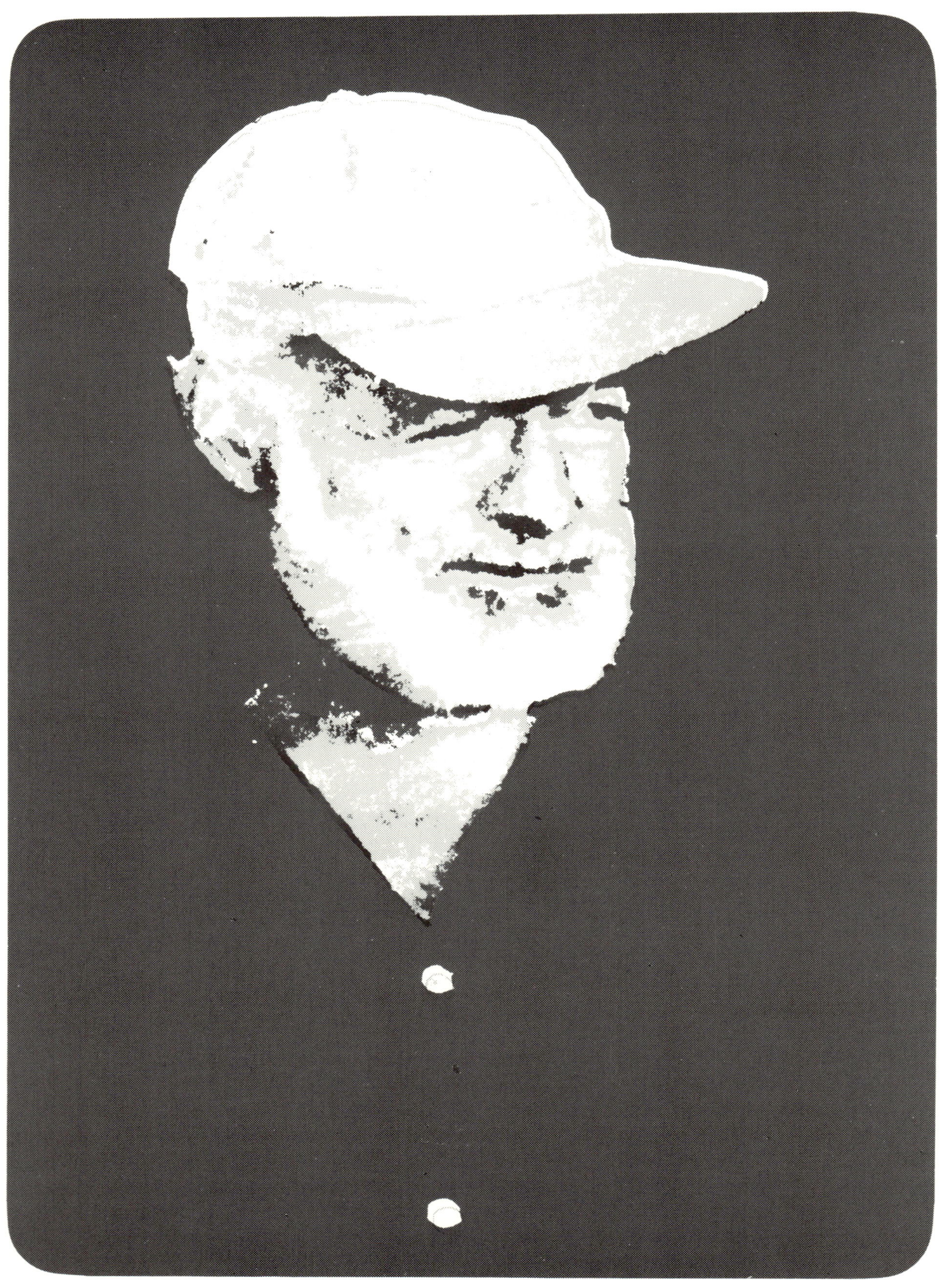

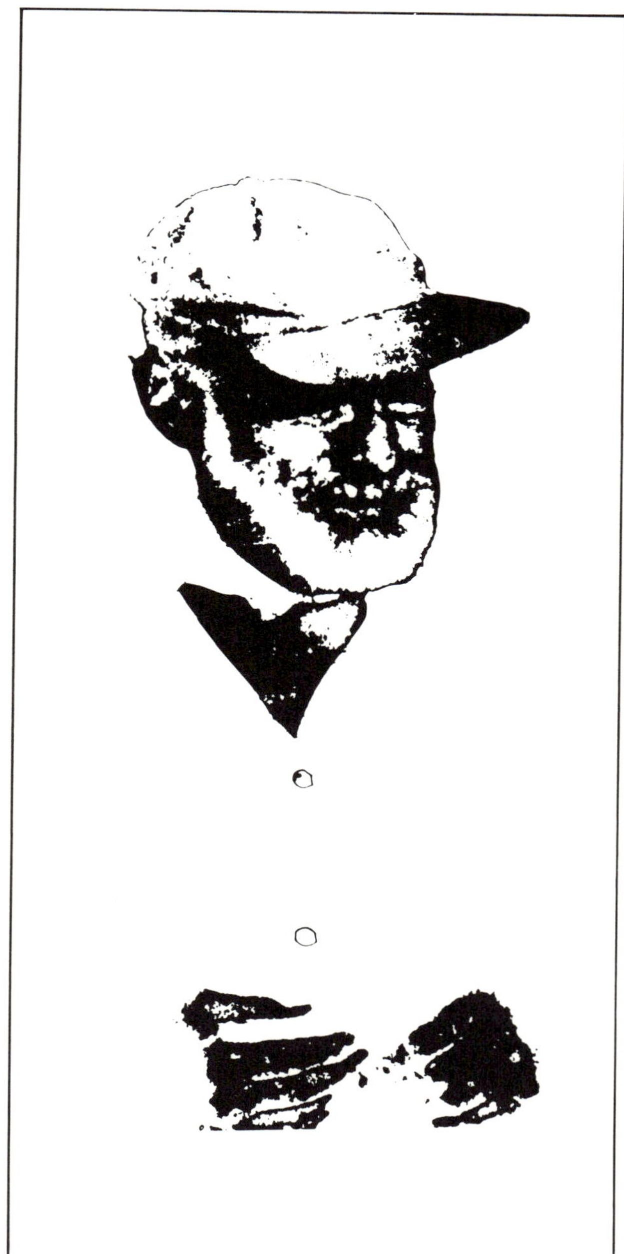 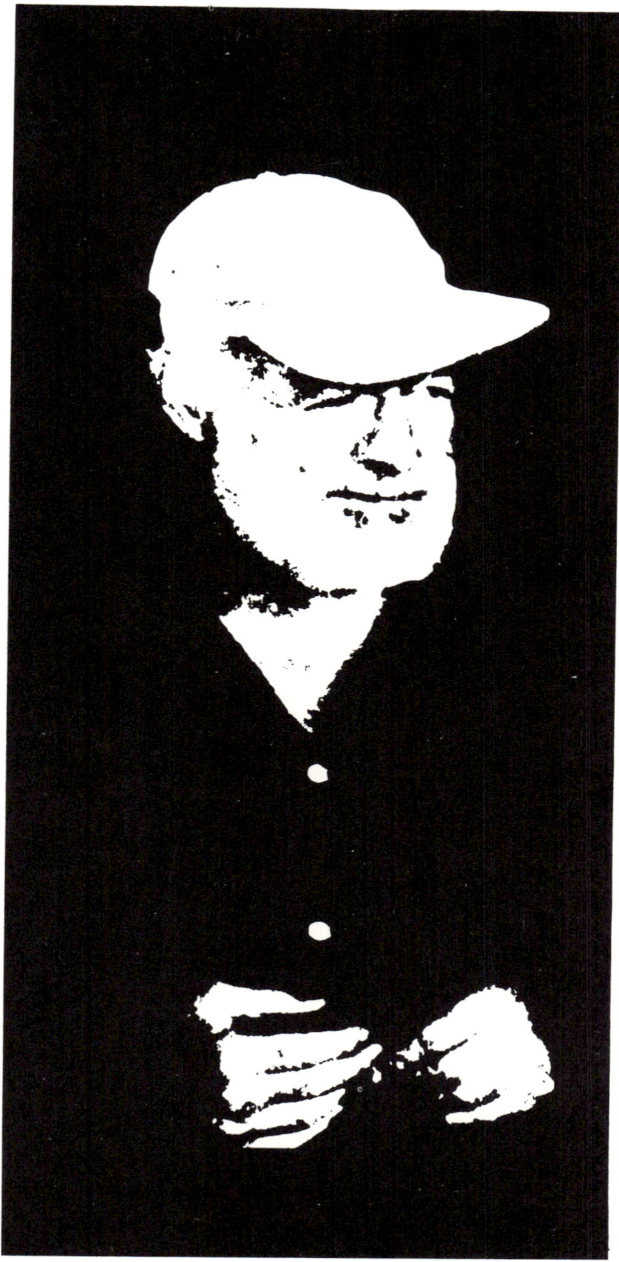

A three-tone separation was used for the jacket illustration of Papa, a biography of Ernest Hemingway. The original image was a snapshot of very poor quality. As you can see, the photoGRAPHIC *transformation is bold and dramatic, and it is simple to print.*

To help you visualize the effect of tone-separation masks is a print (above left) made with only white and black masks. In the original book jacket, the single middle-tone areas revealed in this image were printed in light blue.

In the print, above right, the white and middle-tone masks were used to show the black-tone separation areas. In fact, on the jacket they were printed in dark blue. The light-tone areas were left white.

TONE SEPARATION MASKS

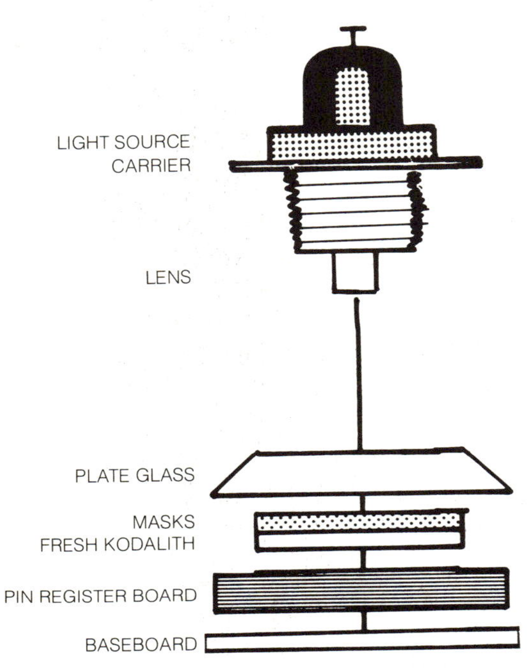

This basic setup is used both to make masks from an original image in the enlarger and to print from masks, using the enlarger as a light source.

Supplies and equipment

Film negative

Enlarger

Safelight, 1A red

Hole punch

Pin register board

Plate glass

Kodalith film, 4″ × 5″ (10 cm × 13 cm)

Kodalith A and B processing chemicals

Instructions

Place the film negative into the carrier of the enlarger, and bring it into focus on the target of the pin register board.

Run a test strip to determine the starting point for the exposures.

Step 1. Expose mask I

When ready to expose, hole punch the sheet of Kodalith, and place it (emulsion side up) on the pin register board. Mask I should have just enough exposure to record the white zone (which corresponds to the gray scale).

Expose and process mask I through to dry.

Step 2. Expose mask II

Place the next hole-punched film on the pin register board, emulsion side up. Next, cover it with mask I, and weight it with glass.

Increase the exposure to accommodate the light gray segment only.

Expose and process mask II through to dry.

Caution: Be certain that the enlarger setup and pin register board are not disturbed during this procedure. If any element accidentally becomes misaligned, causing a loss of registration, you will have to throw everything away and start over again.

Step 3. Expose mask III

Hole punch the third film, and place it on the pin register board. Put mask II on top of it, followed by mask I. Weight the packet with the plate glass. Now increase the exposure time so that the dark-gray area is picked up.

Expose and process mask III through to dry.

Note: Check each mask carefully to see that it contains only the desired density slice of the original image. Use your judgment. This process gives you a lot of leeway; it is not mathematically or mechanically precise. Even if you make a mistake somewhere along the line, you can backtrack a little. Just remake any mask as necessary, and continue.

When the first three steps are completed correctly, you are ready for the final stage.

Step 4.   Expose mask IV

Hole punch another sheet of Kodalith film. Place it on the pin register board. Stack mask III, mask II, and mask I on top of each other—*in that order*. Weight the packet with the plate glass.

This time remove the film negative from the carrier of the enlarger.

Expose with the enlarger light for the brief amount of time determined above.

Process through to dry.

What we have done is to separate a full-range continuous-tone image into four component parts. Each part is in one of the four films. One film contains the white zone, one the light-gray zone, another the dark-gray zone, and the fourth, the black zone. The reason we did not need film in the carrier for the last separation is that the three previous films contained parts of the image. Together they blocked the light from striking any area but the one we wished to be completely black.

The preceding instructions enabled you to create a four-part density separation. Should you wish a three-part separation, simply adjust the exposure accordingly. If your final print calls for five, six, seven, or more tones, just slice the scale into more pieces, controlling the exposure as necessary.

This set of masks will be used in the next chapter, where you will learn how to make a print—they are the key to posterization.

Seven

Printing the Tone Separation Films— Black and White

We now have a stack of four film masks, each representing a single-tone density. We are going to pass white light through the stack three times onto the same sheet of photo paper. The finished print will have solid tones of white, light gray, dark gray, and black, adjacent to each other. The composite effect will be like, and yet unlike, the original photograph. The absence of gradation will give it a totally new look, which is known as *posterization*.

Posterization is a word borrowed from the silk-screen industry. Because of the nature of the silk-screen process and the special paints which only it can use, it is extensively used to manufacture posters. As the silk-screen process is difficult to perform with the conventional halftone method of reproducing photographs, the industry has pioneered the means of posterizing photographs.

The posterized print is made by removing the mask that contains the area we wish to print from the stack. If you want to print black, remove mask IV and then expose for the time that will produce black. Then reassemble the complete stack. For each tone exposure desired, remove only the mask governing that tone and use just enough light to produce that tone.

In black-and-white prints it seems necessary to retain some white areas, because they serve to give authenticity to the black areas and balance to the other tones of the print.

BLACK-AND-WHITE POSTERIZATION

Supplies and equipment

Set of separation film masks

Enlarger, to be used as printing light source

Safelight suitable for the print paper

Sheet of plate glass

Pin register board

Enlarging paper

Paper processing chemicals

Hole punch

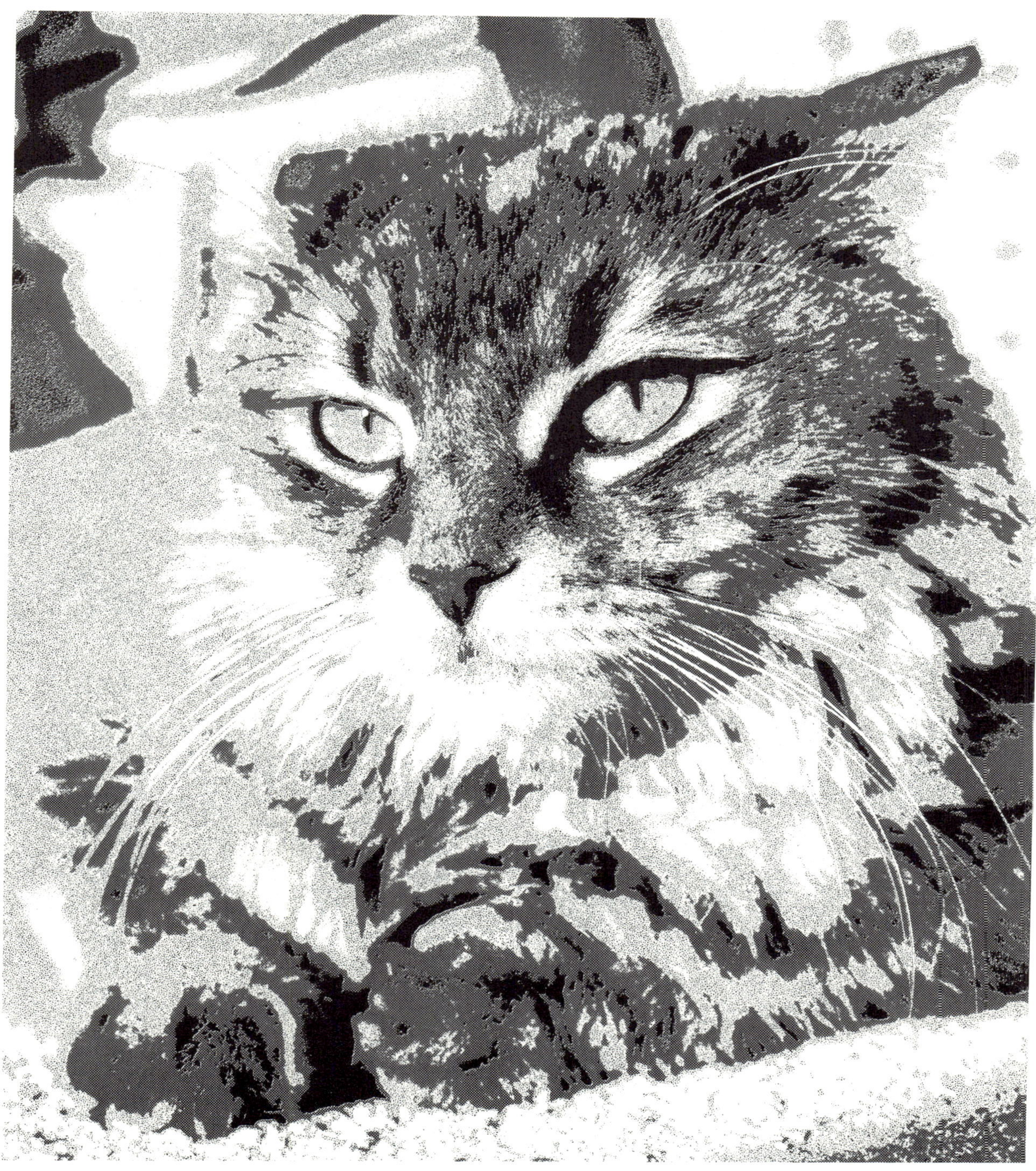

A classic four-tone posterization, made by following the methods explained in this chapter. However, this version goes a step further in that it uses tints.

In the graphic arts, grays of various visual depths can be produced by the use of tints, film screens with an overall dot pattern of a single size. A tint with tiny dots produces a 30 percent gray; a tint with large, heavy dots produces a 90 percent gray that is almost black. Grays can also be simulated by the use of parallel or circular line patterns, mezzotints (simulations of random-grain patterns), and other screens.

To print a tint or other pattern, simply include the appropriate screen at the bottom of the stack of masks (emulsion to emulsion with the photo paper) when you make the exposure for the chosen image tone.

In this cat study, the white is solid (clear; no screen used), the light gray is a 25 percent mezzotint, the dark gray is a 60 percent dot tint, and the black is solid. The black border, applied to the finished print with ruling tape, was chosen for aesthetic reasons.

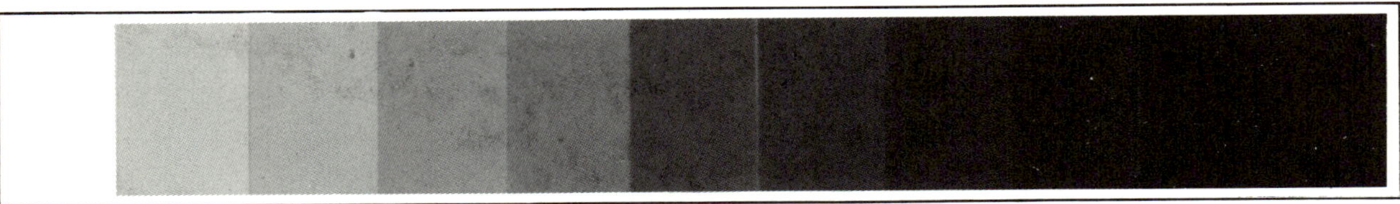

A gray-scale test strip shows the exact exposure time required to produce any tone of gray.

Instructions

Set up the enlarger and pin register board. As we will use the enlarger as a printing light source, check to see that the light covers the printing area. This corresponds to the target area on the pin register board.

To achieve a gray tone on a sheet of black-and-white printing paper, permit just enough light to expose the paper. Now prepare a test strip as we did in Chapter 1. To accurately control the gray tones, there should be a 10- to 20-second spread between the white and black. Adjust the aperture or light intensity to accomplish this.

Using a theoretical exposure scale of white to black in 10 seconds, a light gray is created in 2 seconds, a medium-dark gray in 6 seconds, and a black in 10 seconds. The above exposure time is only an example. Yours may range from 1 to 15 or from 1 to 20 seconds. Select the desired gray, and record its time.

Step 1. *Expose for light gray*

Hole punch the printing paper, and tape it to the pin register board. Assemble the tone-separation masks emulsion side down, with mask I closest to the paper and stack masks II, III, and IV on top of I. To print light gray, remove mask II from the stack. Put the other three masks over the paper on the pin register board, weight with plate glass, and expose. You will have determined from the test strip that a light gray is produced by an exposure of 2 seconds. Therefore, 2 seconds is the correct exposure time.

Step 2. *Expose for dark gray*

Do not disturb the taped print paper. Replace mask II in the stack, and remove mask III. Place the stack of film over the print paper on the pin register board, weight with plate glass, and expose for the dark-gray tone. Check the test strip. It should say 6 seconds.

Step 3. *Expose for black*

Replace mask III, and remove mask IV. Place the stack of film over the paper on the pin register board, weight with plate glass, and expose. The test strip should give you the correct exposure time of 10 seconds for black.

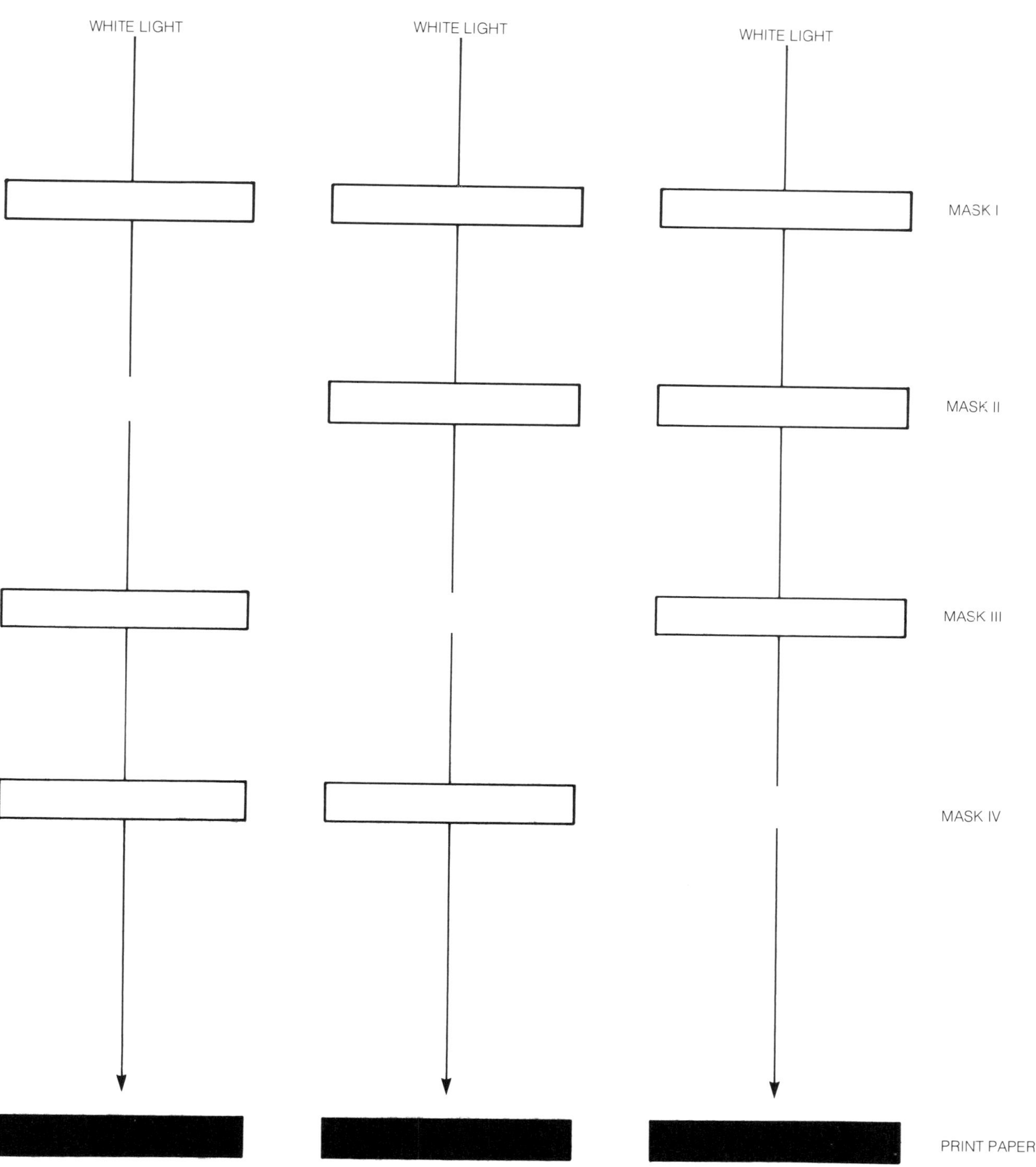

When white is solid, as is usually the case in black-and-white graphics work, only three exposures are required to print a four-tone posterization. At each step, remove the mask of the tone or area you want to print. The remaining masks will block the light; the exposure time will determine the density of the grays and the black. Use the gray-scale test strip to establish the required exposures for the desired densities.

Step 4. Process the print
Once you have made the exposure for black, process the print. Carry it through to wash and dry.

Review what you have done: You started with a full-range continuous-tone image, which you sliced into segments and put together again as *flat* tones. Since these grays were produced under an enlarger on photographic paper, they simulate the solid grays of silk-screen printing and paints. The result — a posterization.

In the graphic arts, grays of various visual depths can be produced by the use of *tints*, film screens with an overall uniform dot pattern. A tint with tiny dots produces a 30 percent gray; a tint with large, heavy dots produces a 90 percent gray that is almost black. Grays can also be simulated through the use of parallel or circular line patterns, mezzotints (simulations of random grain patterns), and other screens.

To print a tint or other pattern, simply include the appropriate screen at the bottom of the stack of masks, emulsion to emulsion to the printing paper. Most of the tints used for these illustrations were made by the Bychrome Company. Tints are produced photographically and can be purchased from graphic arts supply houses. A large variety of patterns from which you can make tints are available from the art materials supply houses. Chartex, Letraset, and Normatone manufacture screens and patterns that can be photographed, sized, and used as photographic tints.

Printing the Tone Separation Films—Color

To make a posterization print in color utilizes essentially the same technique you have just mastered for black and white. In addition you will need some experience in handling and processing color-print paper.

This step is quite simple. Substitute color-print paper for black-and-white paper. Use any brand of color-print paper with compatible chemistry (look at the instructions that come with the paper). Think of black and white as one color. Color paper is composed of three dye layers, which are responsive to the three primary colors. As these colors blend with each other, they produce secondary and tertiary colors and, therefore, have almost unlimited color potential.

A color enlarger is not necessary. A black-and-white one can serve just as well as a white light source. For our purposes at this stage, it is sufficient to know that by passing white light through a color filter onto color paper, we can produce whichever solid color we choose. Its lighter or darker tones can be controlled by exposure, more or less, as we please.

The tricolor filters are red, green, and blue.

	Kodak	
Filter	**Wratten #**	**Prints**
Red	#25	Cyan
Green	#99	Magenta
Blue	#98	Yellow

Place the filter under the lens of the enlarger. Run a series of test strips on color paper. On the segments, carefully mark the filter used and the exposure time. After you have run all necessary tests and have decided just what colors you will use for each of the four areas, you are ready to make a color posterization print.

In black-and-white posterization we kept the white area white. With color posterization we have a choice: white can become pale blue, yellow, pink, light green, and so on. You can also substitute shades of a single color for the white, light gray, dark gray, or black masks. The possibilities for multicolor effects are as wide as your imagination.

To save time in getting into color work, use the set of tone separation masks from Chapter 6. Once you have

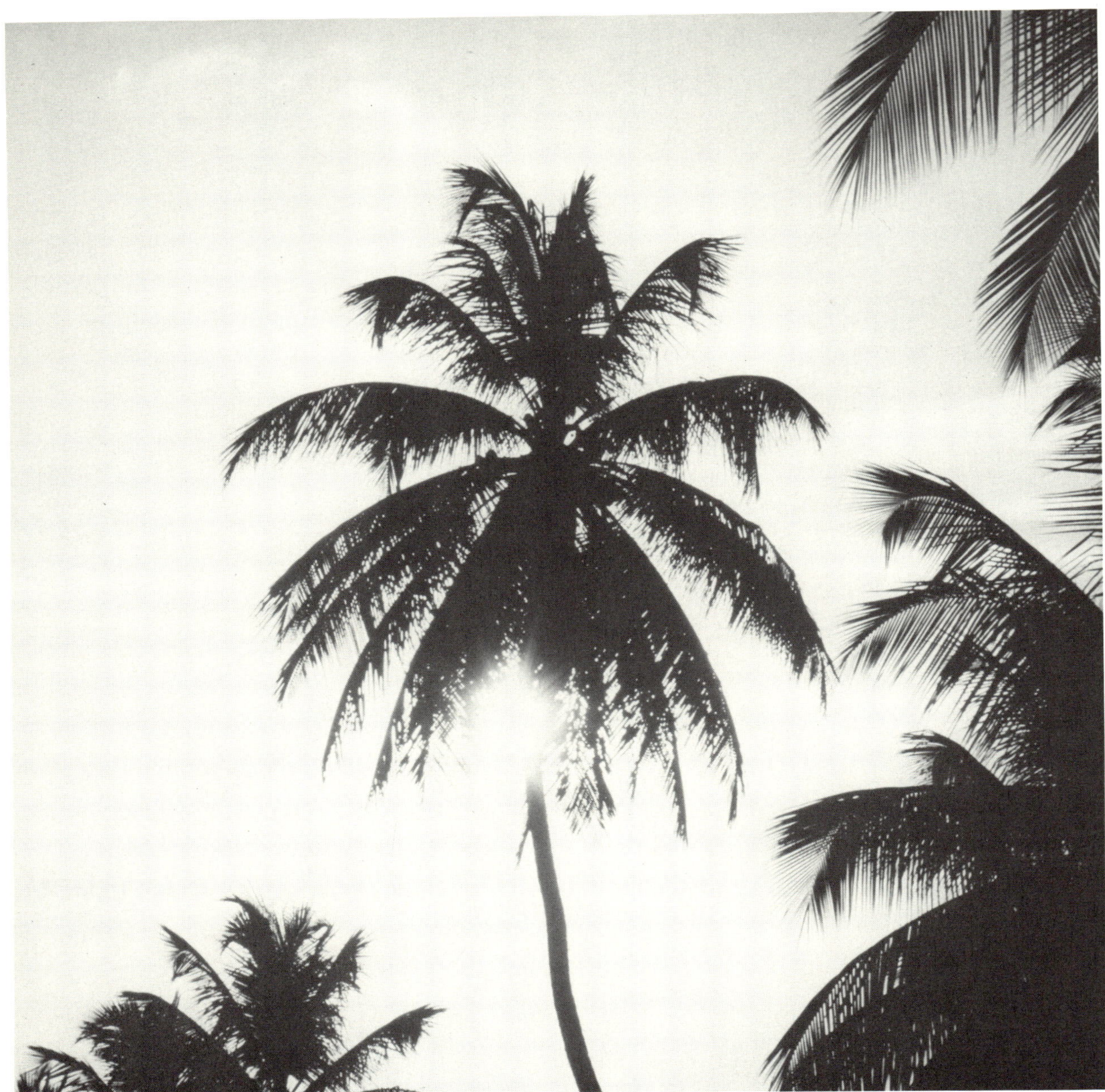

Here is a comparison between a tone print, above, and its black-and-white posterization, right. The posterized image includes an interesting variation: mask II for the light-gray area has been reversed. That is, the mask was made in the usual way, then contact printed on Kodalith to produce its opposite. The opposite mask produced the background gray. The gap between mask II and the black of mask IV creates an interesting drop-out effect.

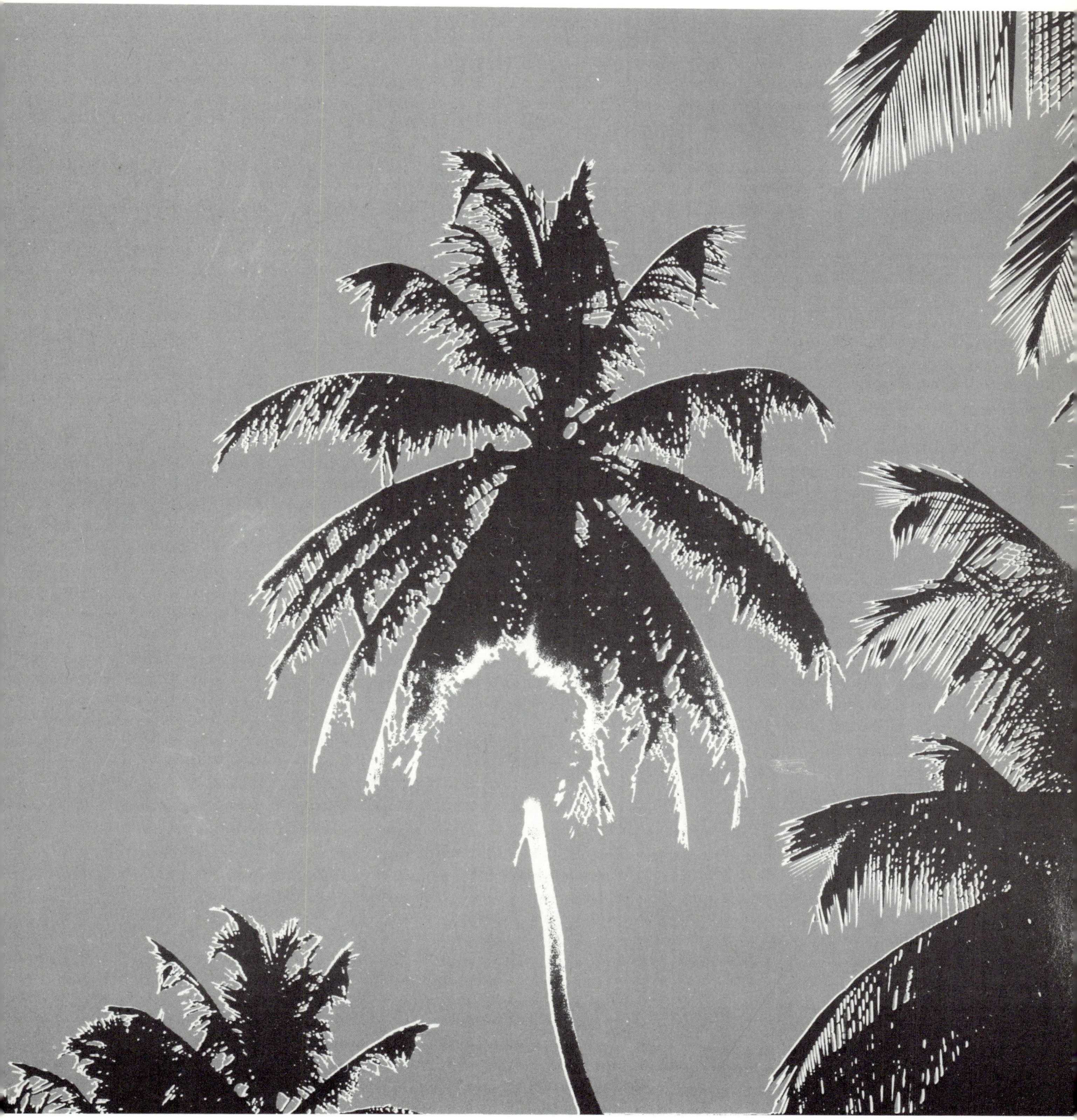

mastered the techniques of color, you can select another subject. As you do the slicing, think of each slice as a color, rather than as light gray, dark gray, or black.

COLOR POSTERIZATION

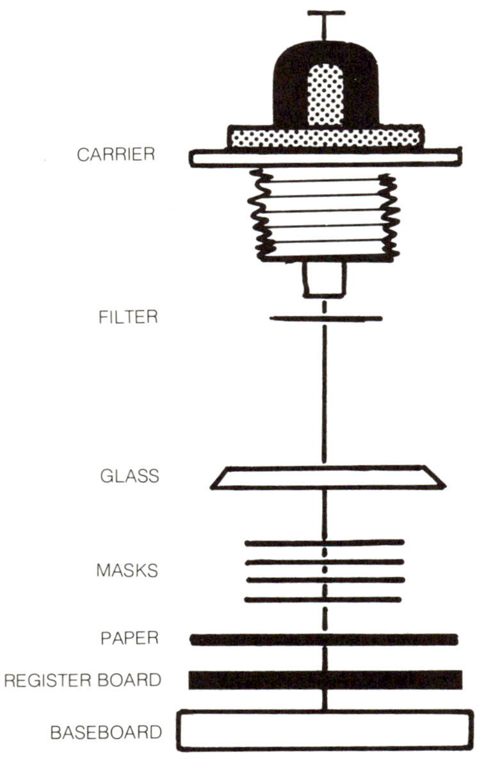

In printing color posterizations, a red, blue, or green filter is used over the lens to produce cyan, yellow, or magenta. Other colors can be produced by successive exposures through two different filters. Different filters must be used each time the mask sequence is changed or the two separation levels will be the same color.

Supplies and equipment

Set of separation masks

Set of tricolor filters

Enlarger, to be used as printing light source

Pin register board

Plate glass

Color print paper

Color paper processing chemicals

Hole punch

Masking tape

Instructions

Set up the enlarger and pin register board following the instructions given in Chapter 7 for the black-and-white print.

Check: That the light covers the target area.

Check: That the pin register board is taped to the baseboard.

Check: That some device holds the tricolor filters securely under the lens.

Because all of the exposures will be carried out in *total darkness*, it's wise to place everything you will need in a handy position before you begin. Avoid losing an hour's work because of some mishap, such as using the same filter twice or dropping something on the floor.

Since you will have to remove some masks and replace them with others while performing the successive exposures, you must be able to distinguish one from the other. The solution to this problem is to *edge notch* the masks. To do this, cut a number of V's corresponding to the mask number (see the illustration):

Mask I	V
Mask II	VV
Mask III	VVV
Mask IV	VVVV

Option: You may prefer, instead, to make half holes or U's with a stationery punch.

It is customary to notch the right-hand corner of the film. That way, when you're handling the masks in total darkness, you can conveniently identify them with your right index finger.

Check: That the glass is clean.

Check: That the filters are edge-notched, so you can tell red, green, and blue apart in the dark. (As an alternative you can snip a small piece from one, two, or three corners for ready identification.)

Masks (and filters) can be edge notched to ensure correct identification by touch in the dark.

Timing Chart

Zone	Color Choice	Filter	Time
I white	pale yellow	blue	2 sec.
II light gray	light magenta	green	2 sec.
III dark gray	medium cyan	red	5 sec.
IV black	strong green	red +	5 sec. +
		blue	5 sec.

This timing chart is offered only as an example—to ensure accuracy you must make your own. Do it by making a series of step-exposure test strips, following the same procedure you used to make a gray-scale test strip. Make a separate test strip through each filter so you will know how many seconds is required to achieve an intensity of cyan, magenta, or yellow. Use the enlarger light at the same height as for printing. Note carefully what f-stop is required to get a usable range of exposures (at least 1– 10 seconds).

Notice in the sample timing chart that the mask IV exposure is actually two equal exposures through two separate filters. That's one way to get primary and secondary colors.

Color Filter Chart

Filters	Print color
Red	Cyan
Green	Magenta
Blue	Yellow
Red and Blue	Green
Blue and Green	Red
Red and Green	Blue
Red and Green and Blue	Black

Important points

1. You cannot expose through two filters at the same time. If you do so, the filters will block all the light, and there will be no exposure.

2. Equal exposures through two filters will produce red, green, or blue. Unequal exposures will produce variant

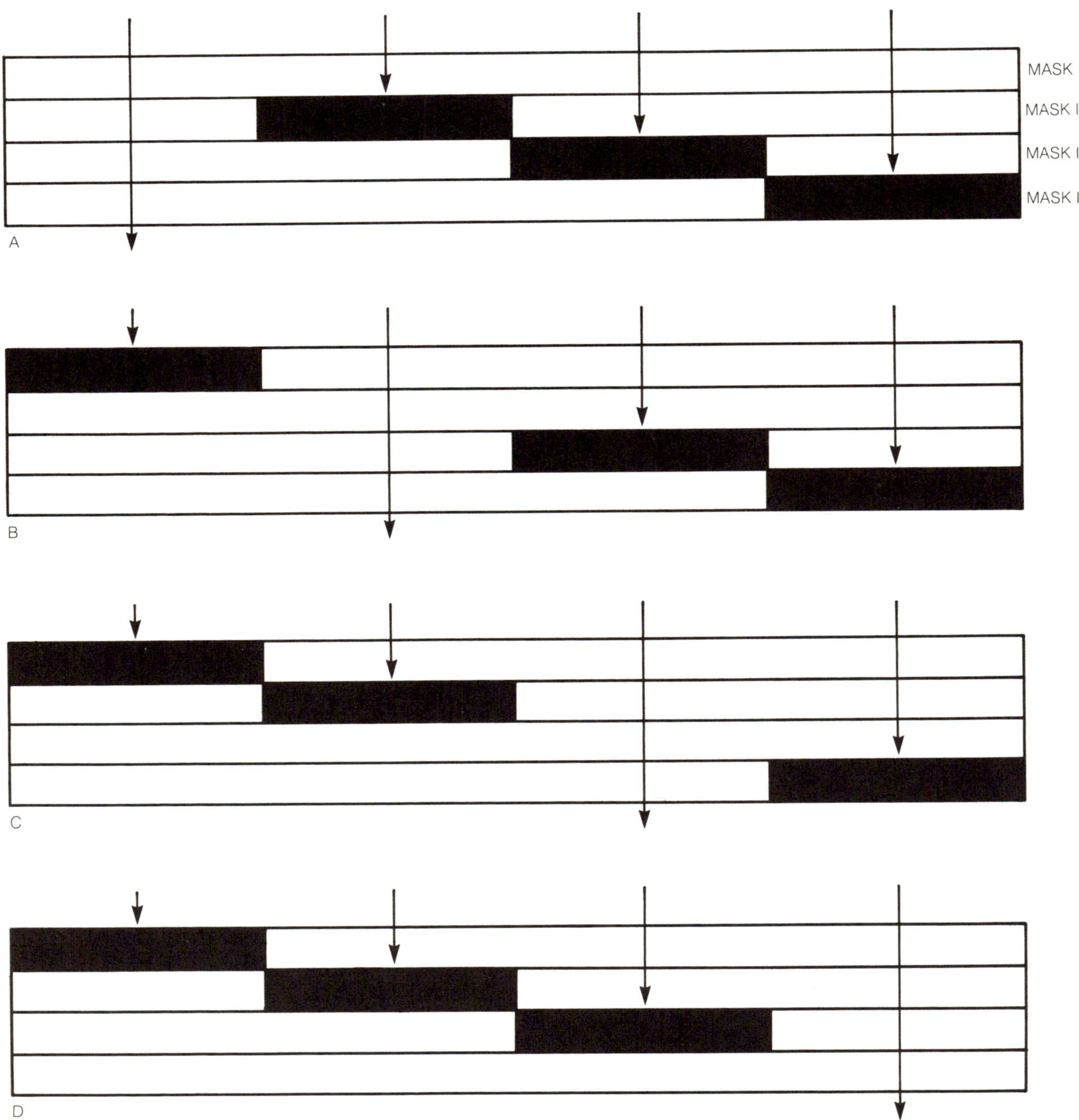

Here is the mask-shifting sequence for four-color posterization. For the sake of clarity, the position of the mask removed to print each area has been indicated:
A. *To print lightest tone (white) areas*
B. *To print medium-light areas*
C. *To print medium-dark areas*
D. *To print darkest (black) areas*

colors, such as lime green, orange, and violet. Later, you can do some controlled tests to discover these colors; now is not the time.

3. Remember to change the filter or the exposure each time the mask sequence is changed or the two separation levels will be the same color.

Step 1.   *Expose for white zone — mask I*
Hole punch a sheet of color-print paper. Place it in position on the pin register board, and tape it securely. After having removed mask I, place the stack of masks, emulsion side down, on the color-print paper. Weight with plate glass. Place the filter in position, and expose according to the color intensity you selected on the timing chart.

Step 2.   *Expose for light-gray zone — mask II*
Replace mask I. Remove mask II. Place the stack of masks on the color paper on the pin register board. Weight with plate glass. Remove the blue filter, replace it with the green filter, and expose.

Step 3.   *Expose for dark-gray zone — mask III*
Replace mask II. Remove mask III. Place the stack back on the pin register board, and weight with glass. Remove the green filter. Replace it with the red, and expose.

Step 4.   *Expose for the black zone — mask IV*
Replace mask III. Remove mask IV. Place the stack back on the pin register board. Weight with glass. Leave the red filter in position, and expose.

Step 5.   *Expose for mask IV again*
Remove the red filter. Replace it with blue. LEAVE EVERY-THING ELSE ALONE. Expose once again. LET OUT YOUR BREATH!!

Step 6.   *Process the print*
Process the color paper in color-paper chemicals through to dry.

Now that you have succeeded with your first color posterization, you are free to think of variations. How, for example, would it look if the colors were used in a different order? Set up a new exposure timing chart, and start on your second print. Remember, you must always make up your own test strips and record the colors. The color guides you make will help you to reproduce the color values whenever you want them.

If you have followed the instructions offered in this chapter carefully you will have mastered a fundamental technique. Continue to work carefully, step by step, to explore its potential — there are virtually no limits to the color combinations you can make!

Continue using the 4″ × 5″ (10 cm × 13 cm) film size. At this point, it is not a limitation. With a little ingenuity you can enlarge the negatives in register, or, you may prepare a set of original masks in 8″ × 10″ (20 cm × 25 cm), 11″ × 14″ (28 cm × 36 cm), or 16″ × 20″ (41 cm × 51 cm). To do this is quite practical and easy.

Part Two:
MORE IDEAS

Earlier chapters explained the basic ways of working with high-contrast materials. They show how these types of images are *made*. The illustrations in the following section are meant to show some of the creative possibilities offered by the previously explained techniques and what you can *do* with these materials and methods. These illustrations are meant to provide inspiration by demonstrating some of the ways the techniques (or a combination of techniques) can be applied to your own images.

It is important to remember that it is the photographer who creates an interesting and important picture. You cannot rely on an unusual technique alone to produce a good image. It is what you portray in high contrast—the image you choose to alter and in what way—that will make the final picture powerful and valuable—not only to yourself but to others as well.

A number of new elements and techniques (such as contact screens and tints or mirrors) were used in the creation of the following images, but where a new technique is introduced the caption accompanying the picture explains what it is and how it was used.

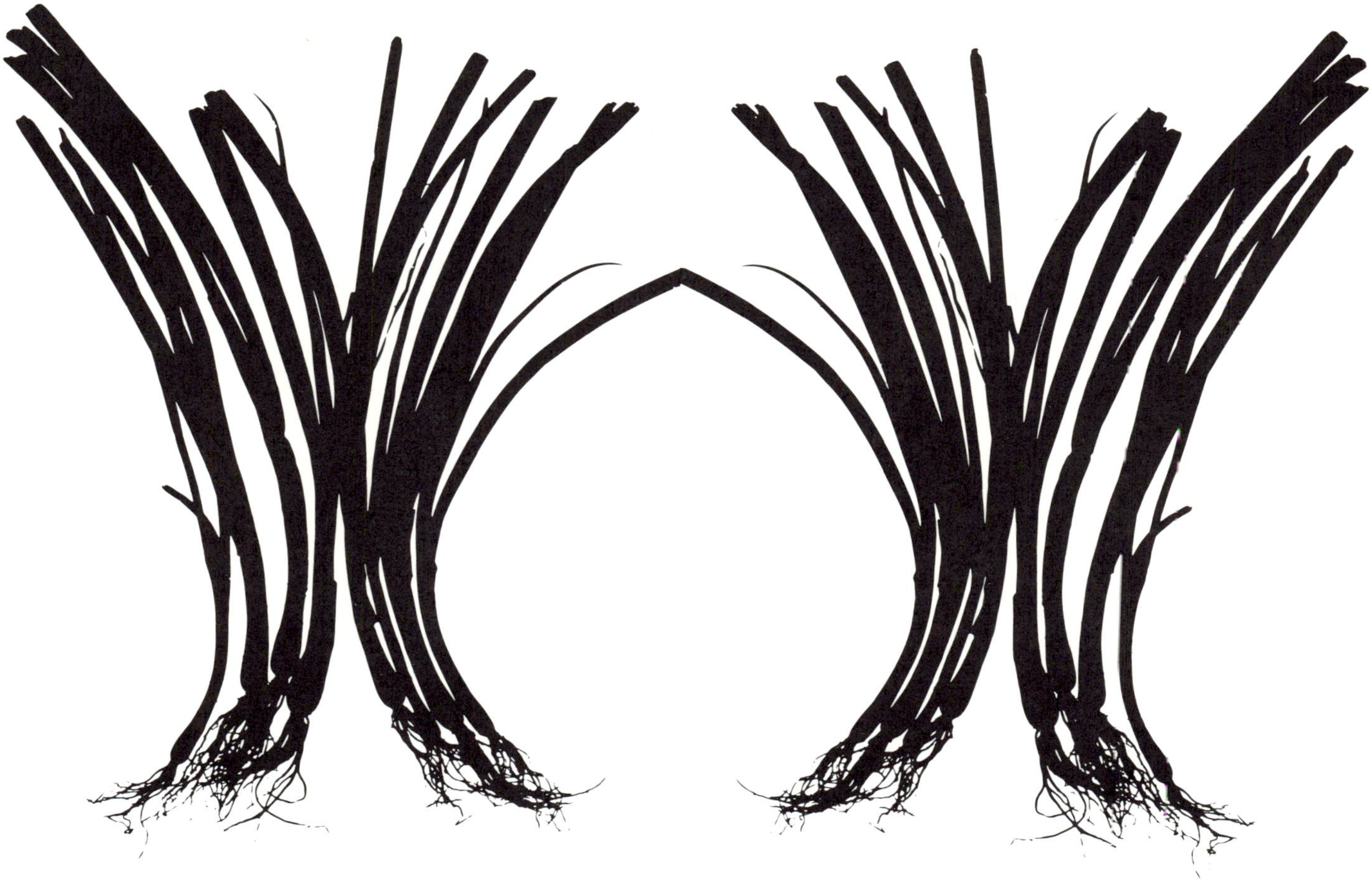

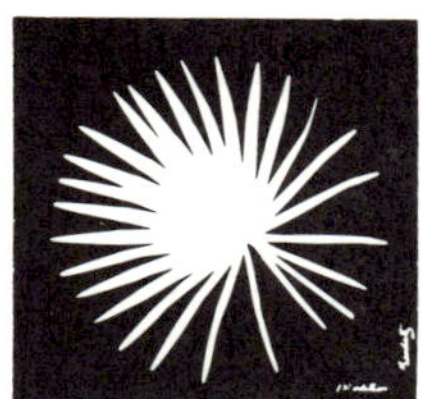 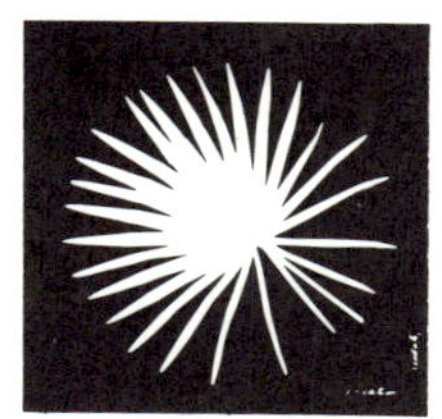 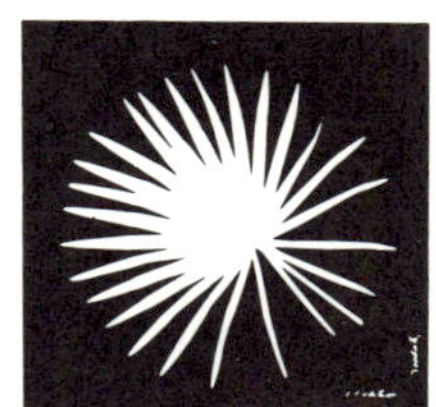 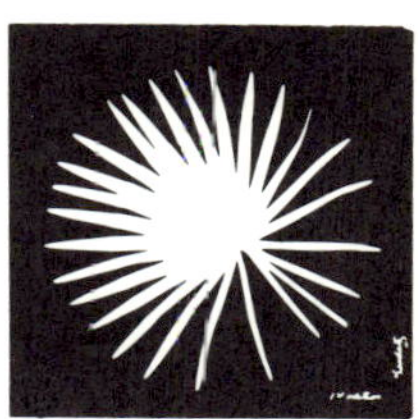

Interesting multiple images can be created from one or two elements. The simplest approaches are repeat and mirror images. These methods are among those used to create commercial designs for textiles, wallpaper, printed paper products, box wraps, and packaging.

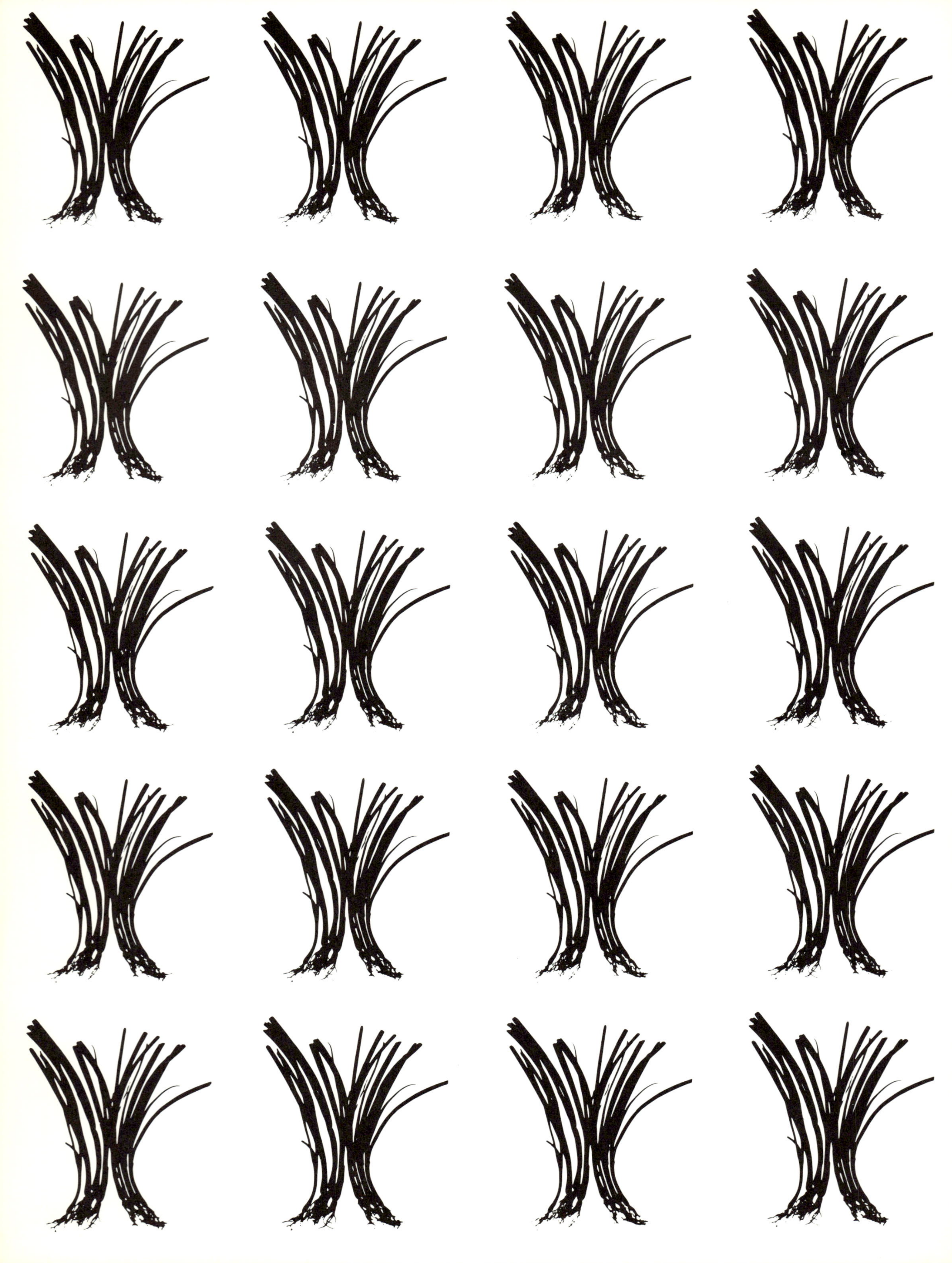

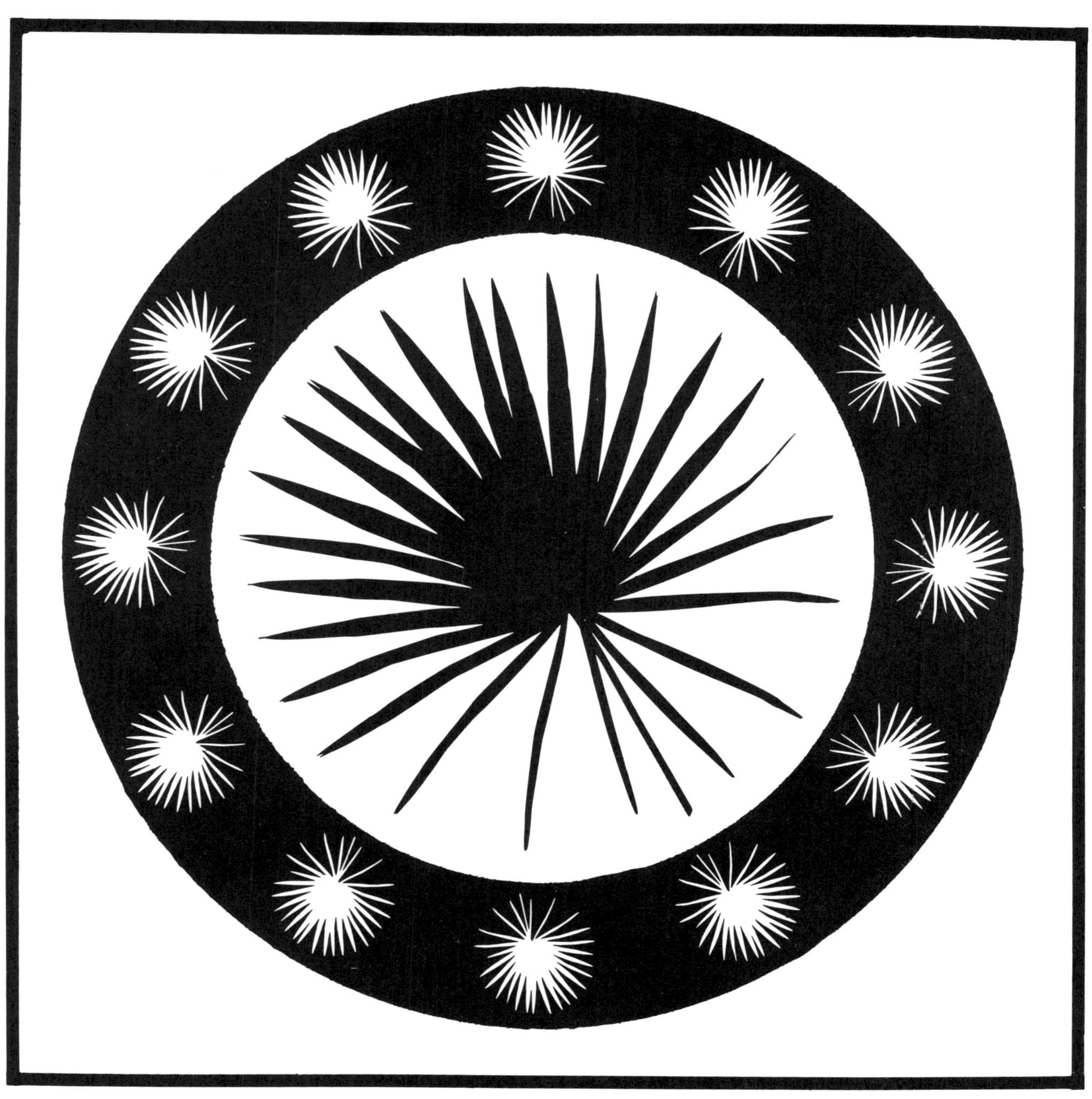

Left. *Step-and-repeat patterns can be created by pasting up multiple copies of an image element. This avoids the problem of starting over from scratch if you make a mistake in a repeated exposure system on a single sheet of paper or film. Prepare a quantity of paper prints and carefully paste them in position on a background board. Touch up the cut edges with white paint, and photograph the final composite.*

Above. *Repeats can be varied in layout, size, and tone. A variation on a theme, such as this one, can be accomplished by cutting and pasting paper prints. An alternative is to use film images on a light box, or multiple exposures on a single frame of film. Consider using opaque masks to protect various parts of the print paper.*

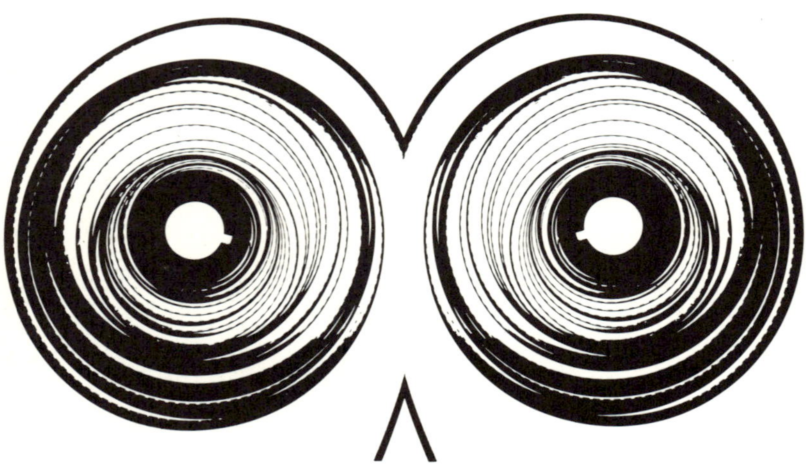

A mirror image is created by printing an element, flopping the original, and printing it again alongside itself, an operation called *unfolding* the image. Mirror patterns can be unfolded vertically, horizontally, diagonally, and in even more complex patterns.

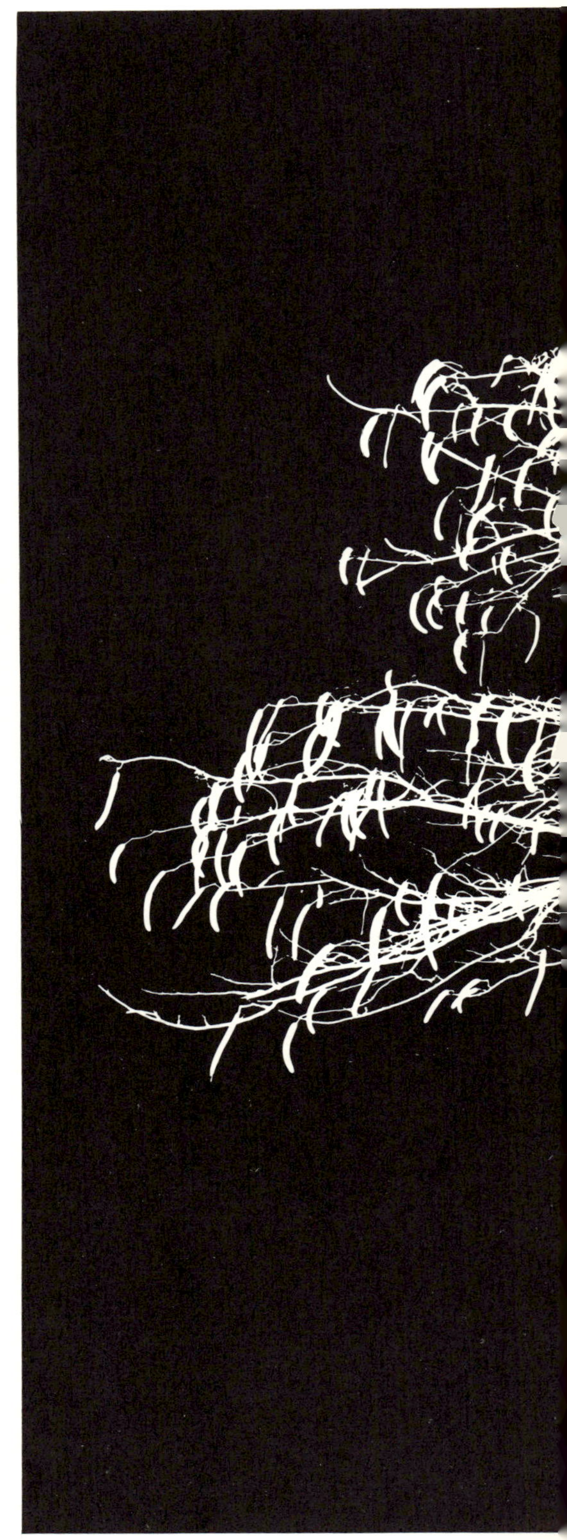

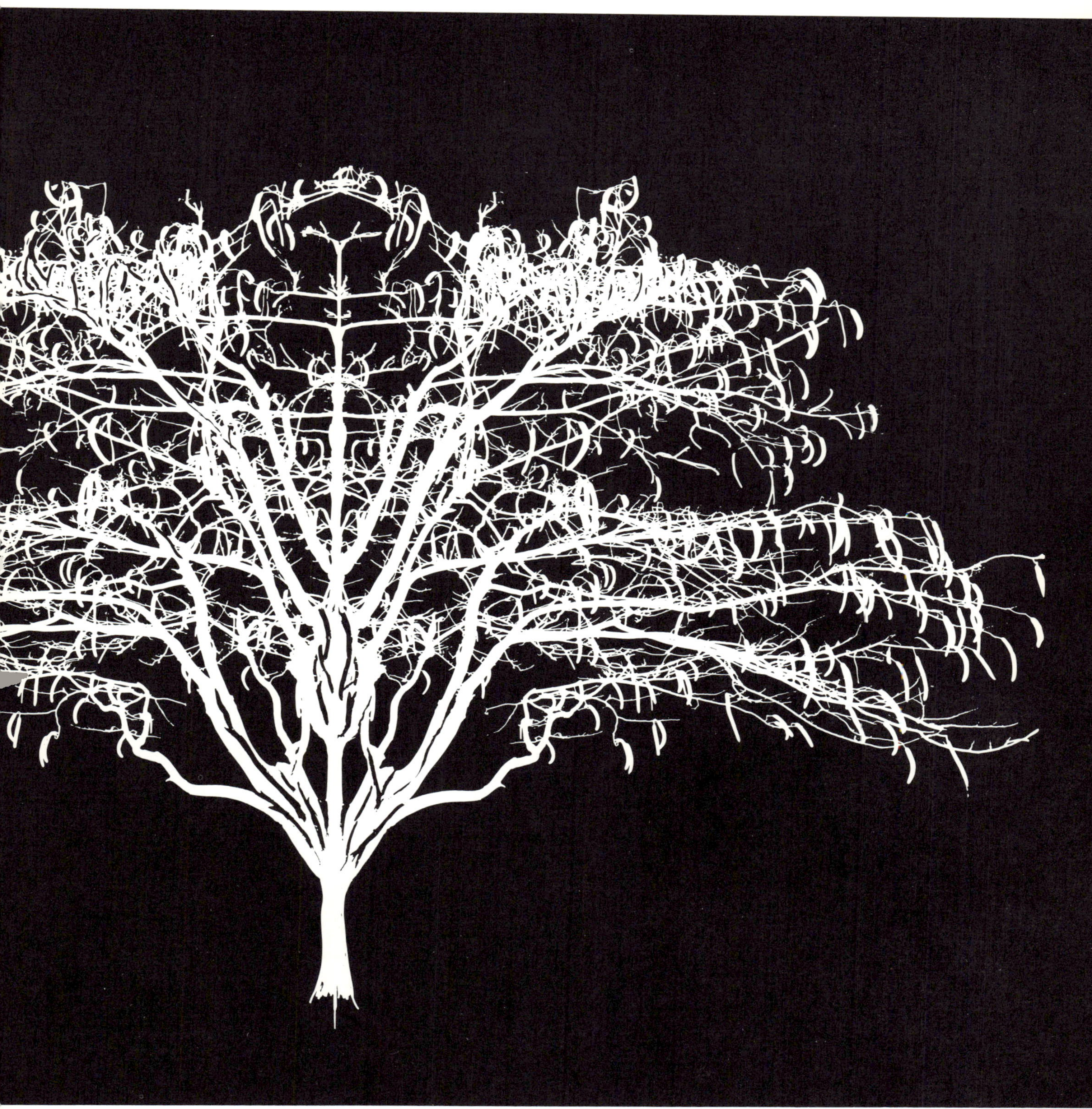

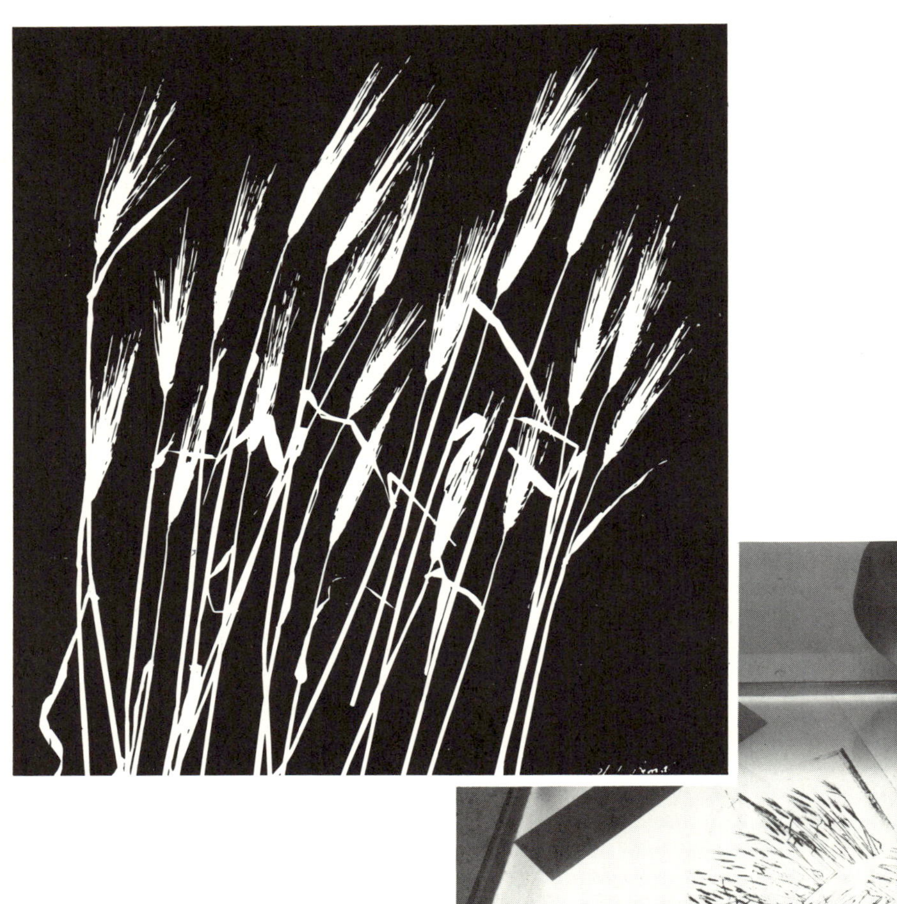

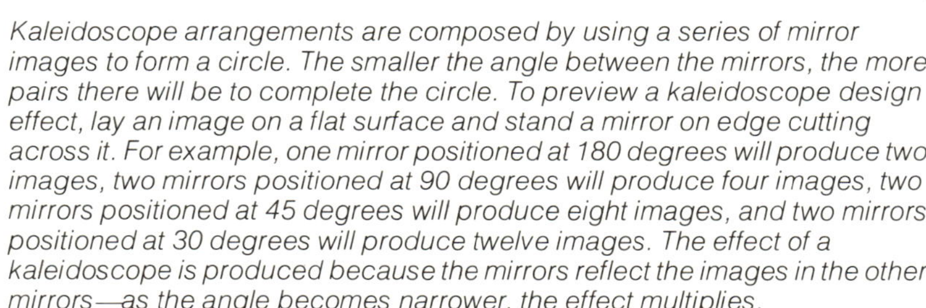

Kaleidoscope arrangements are composed by using a series of mirror images to form a circle. The smaller the angle between the mirrors, the more pairs there will be to complete the circle. To preview a kaleidoscope design effect, lay an image on a flat surface and stand a mirror on edge cutting across it. For example, one mirror positioned at 180 degrees will produce two images, two mirrors positioned at 90 degrees will produce four images, two mirrors positioned at 45 degrees will produce eight images, and two mirrors positioned at 30 degrees will produce twelve images. The effect of a kaleidoscope is produced because the mirrors reflect the images in the other mirrors—as the angle becomes narrower, the effect multiplies.

To produce a kaleidoscopic image photographically, begin by creating a mirror pair. Print each negative twice, once by contact to the emulsion side and once by contact to the base side. The result will be a pair of Kodalith films, which can be joined from any of four sides. To get a clearer idea of what we mean, consider your own hands, which are mirror images of each other. With the palms open, join your two little fingers. Then turn your hands over and join your thumbs—the result is a mirror pair.

Pictured above is the original photogram of barley, and several Kodalith positives made from this image on a light table. They were overlapped and moved around until the desired arrangement was found. The final result, at right, was photographed directly from the arrangement on the light table. Although it looks like the result of complex mirror work, it's not.

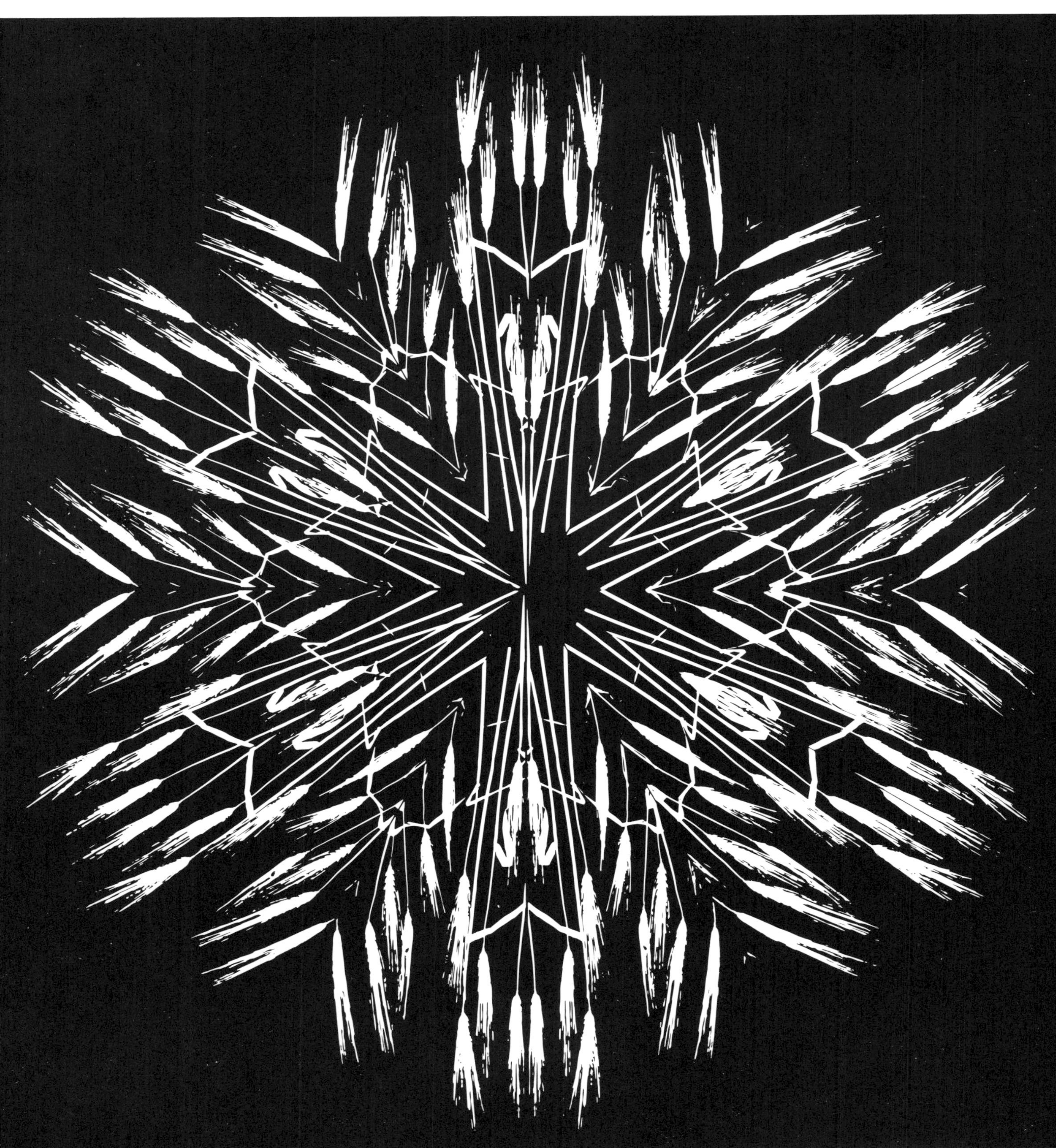

As a variation, consider working with one of the separations, as was done in this image of a female form.

In this print a solid black was needed as a counterpoint to the 25 percent mezzotint gray. The solid white is very minor but is important as an edge line.

Throughout these instructions, there has been a tendency to slice densities by the gray-scale values. In the interest of aesthetics you will find it more effective to guide yourself by the image and not slice everything in a one, two, three, or four-tone treatment.

Spread the separations over a light table, and re-evaluate the final print sequence. Careful study of these may suggest some new and different imagery to you.

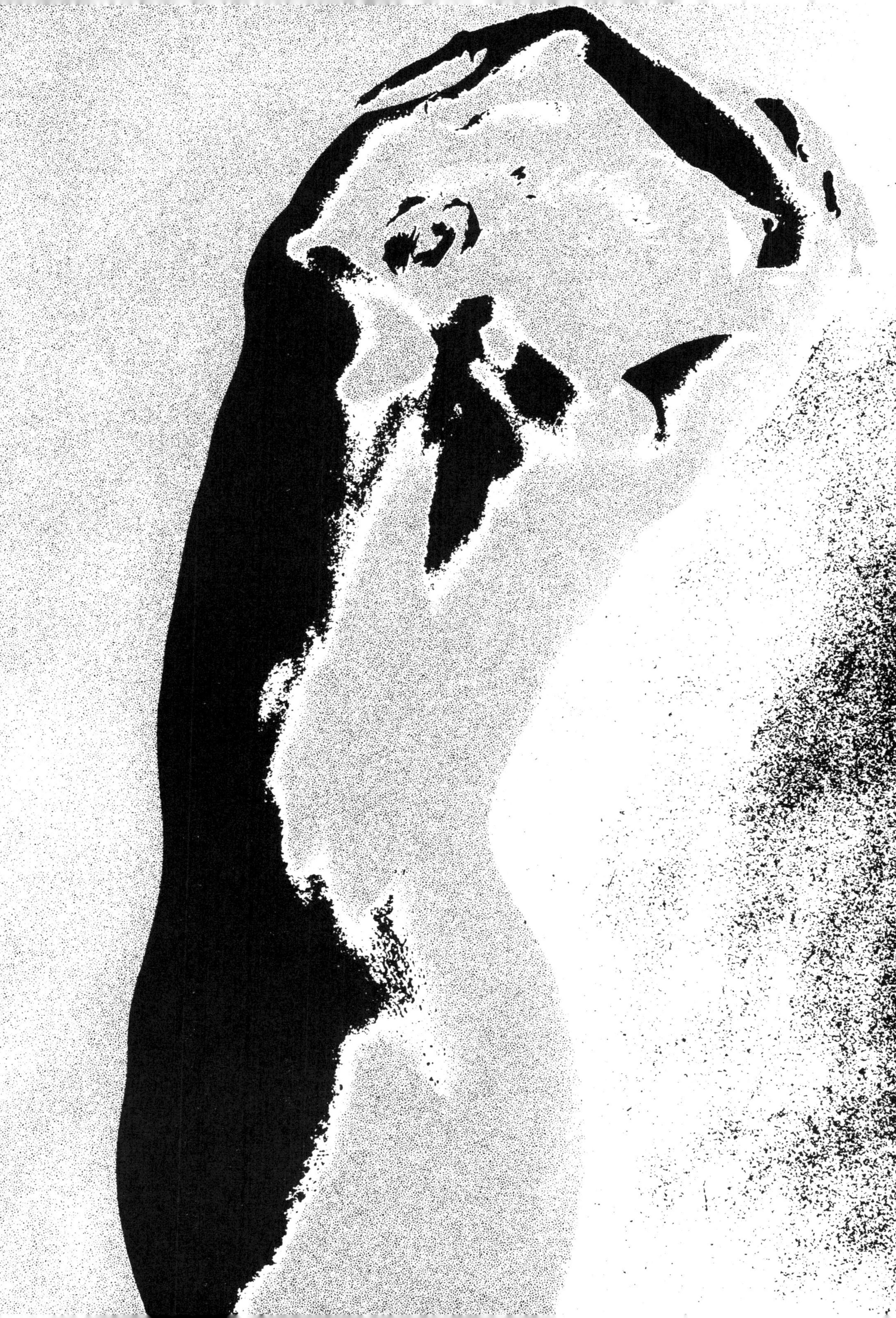

The picture above was created by photographing the tone image of a male form through a fairly coarse halftone screen onto Kodalith, and enlarging it. Dot size varies according to the tone of each area in the original. Viewed close up, the dots are the dominating force. Note the regular pattern of the dot size in the background area and the larger dot size forming the arms, legs, and torso. At 50 percent gray, the round dot shifts to square, as seen at the head.

Placing the image farther away blends the tones, the shift in dot size representing shading and tonality, and a human form emerges. Since this was originally a low-key print, the grays are close to each other. This results in dots of a fairly uniform size.

In the print at right, the scale of contrast is greater than that in the print of the male form. Therefore, the dots have a greater variety of sizes of rounds and squares, and from a distance merge into a fully constructed image with all the nuance of the original continuous-tone print.

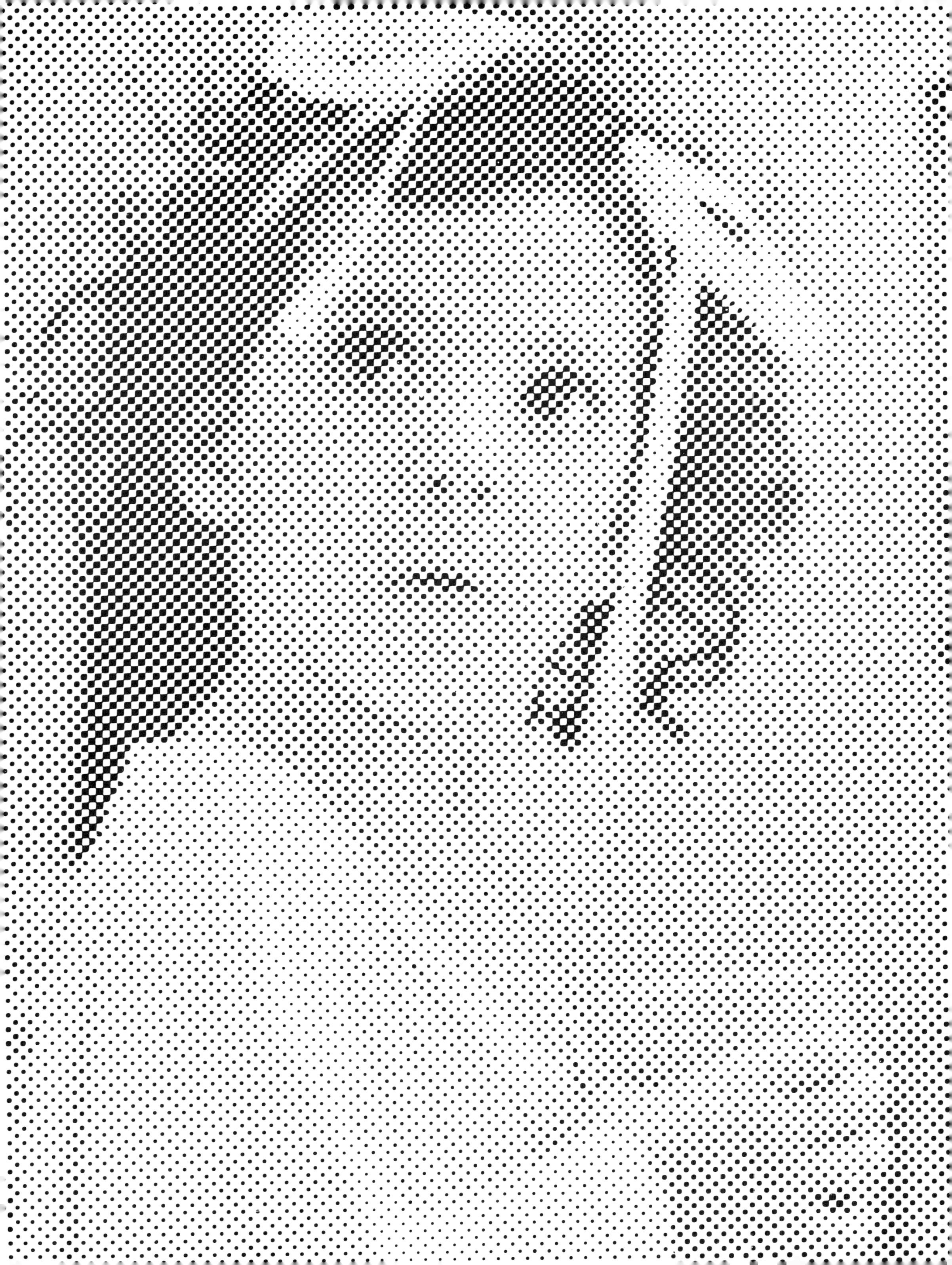

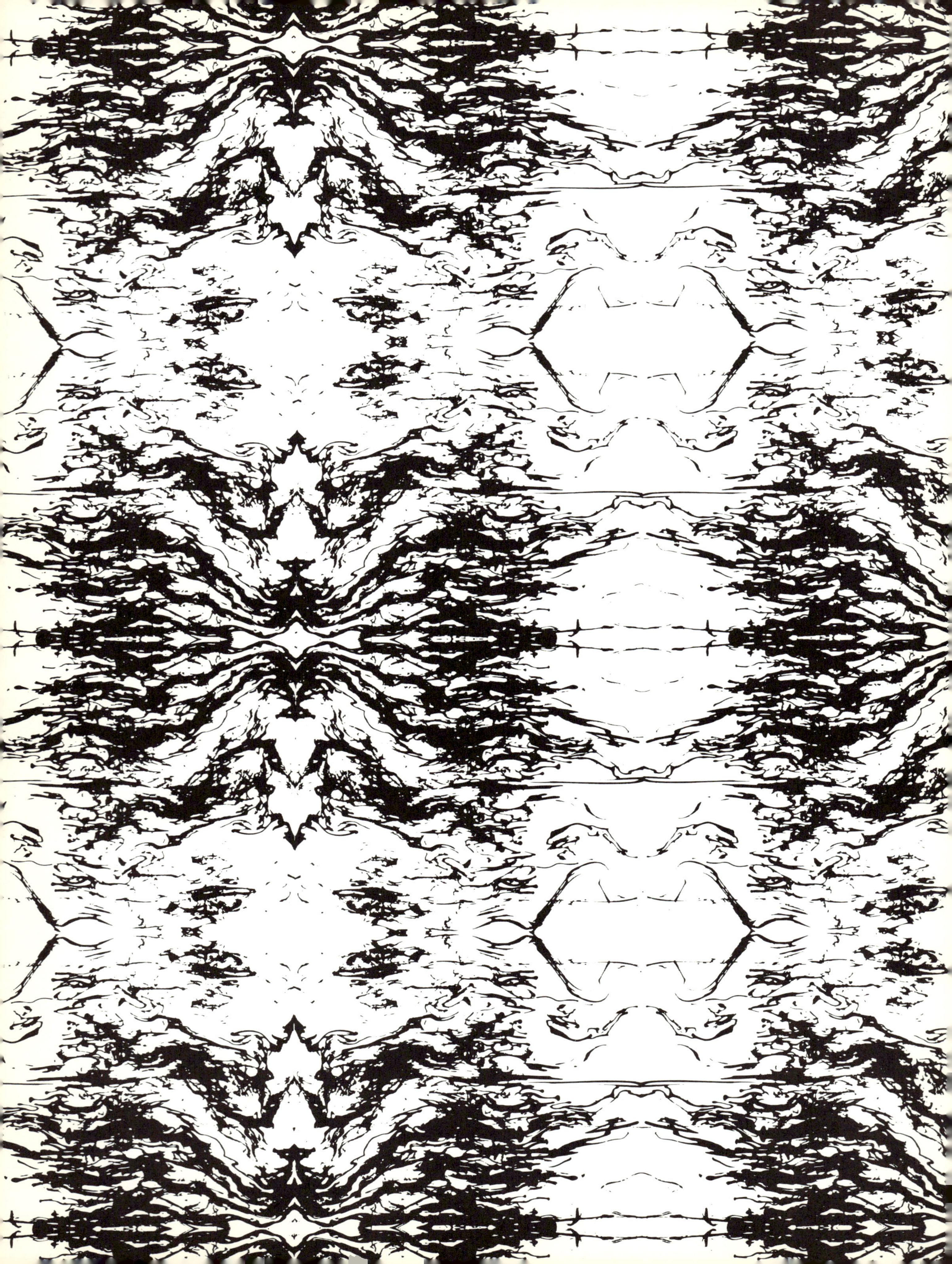

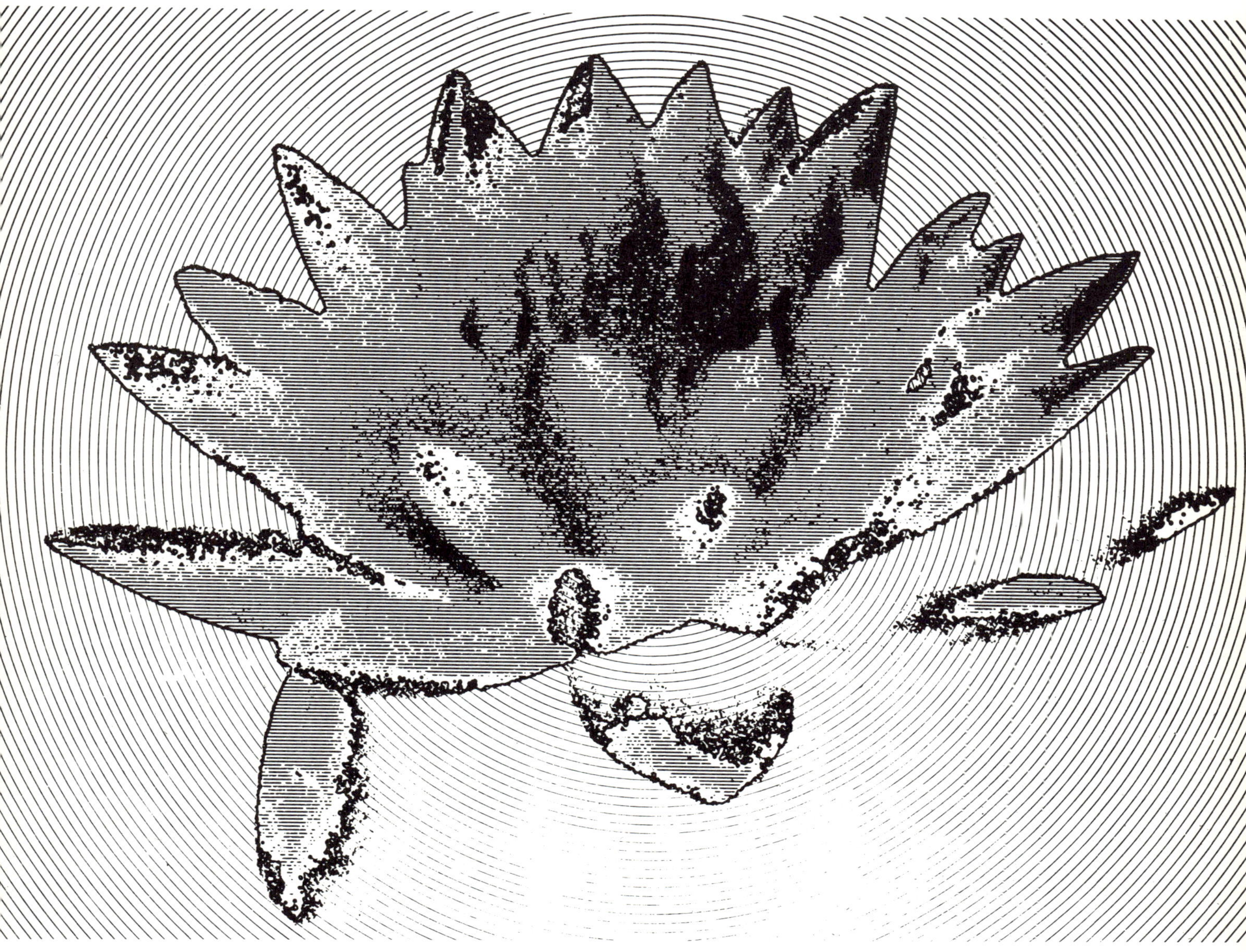

Left. *Some of the images in this section were made in response to a particular project or challenge. Others were made in the spirit of pure curiosity and experimentation. From an amorphous tone-color image came a Kodalith abstraction that really works.*

Ask yourself the following questions: What if the image were unfolded horizontally? What if the image were unfolded vertically? Here are the answers.

Above. *Up until now we have stressed density separation. This image, on the other hand, illustrates area separation. Isolating an area or a motif and accenting it can be done through contrast—placing a light image against a dark one or a dark against a light, or by using a contrasting color. In this case, contrast was achieved with a geometric pattern.*

A circline background was chosen, because we quite naturally visualize a water lily in a pool of water surrounded by concentric ripples. Straightline and circline screens are available in different weights of lines and spacing; they can simulate most values of gray.

This water lily print was made with three exposures, two of which had screen tints added to the separations. Sometimes the subject matter will point you in a particular direction, but it takes some trial and error to finalize the result.

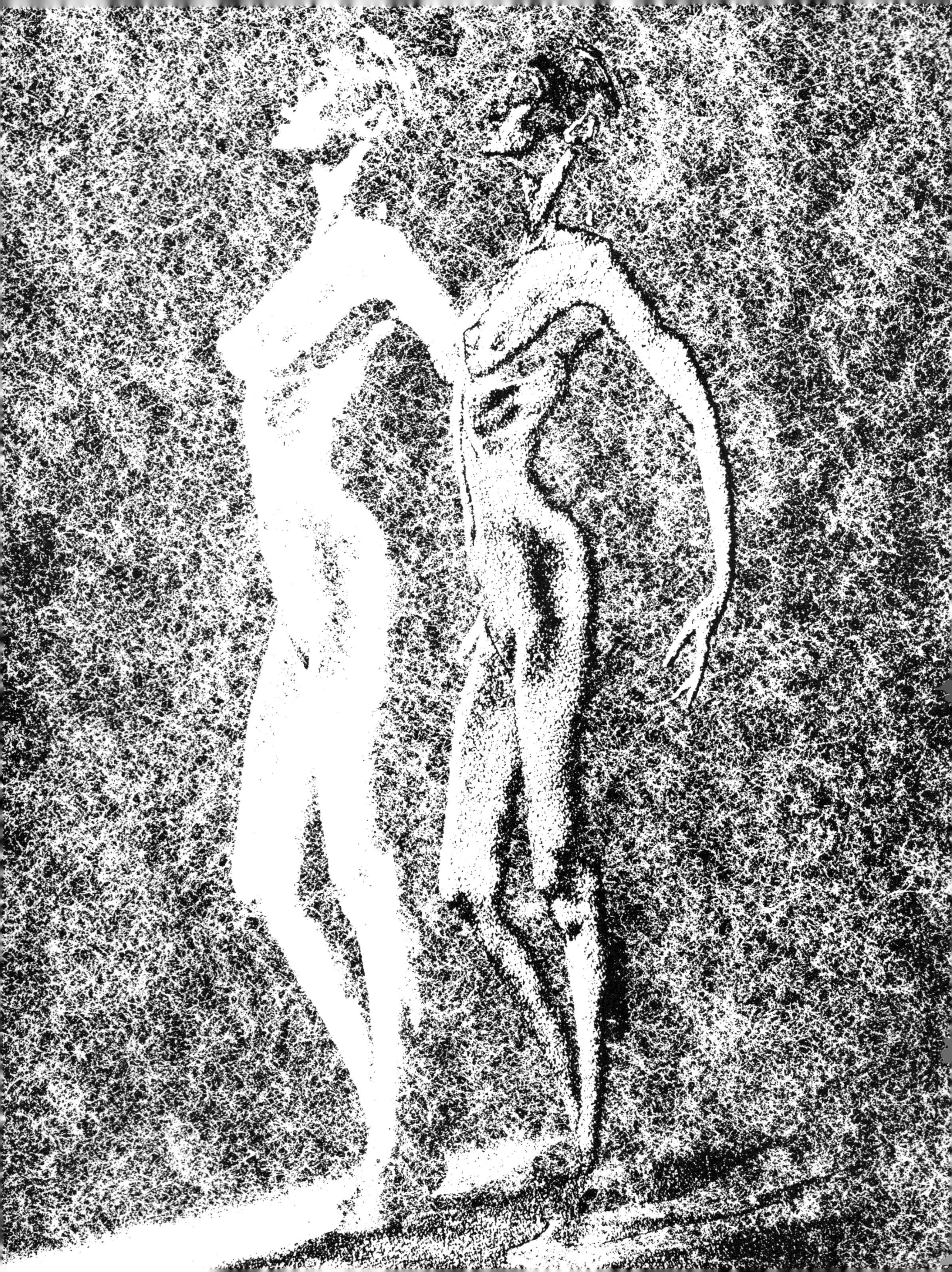

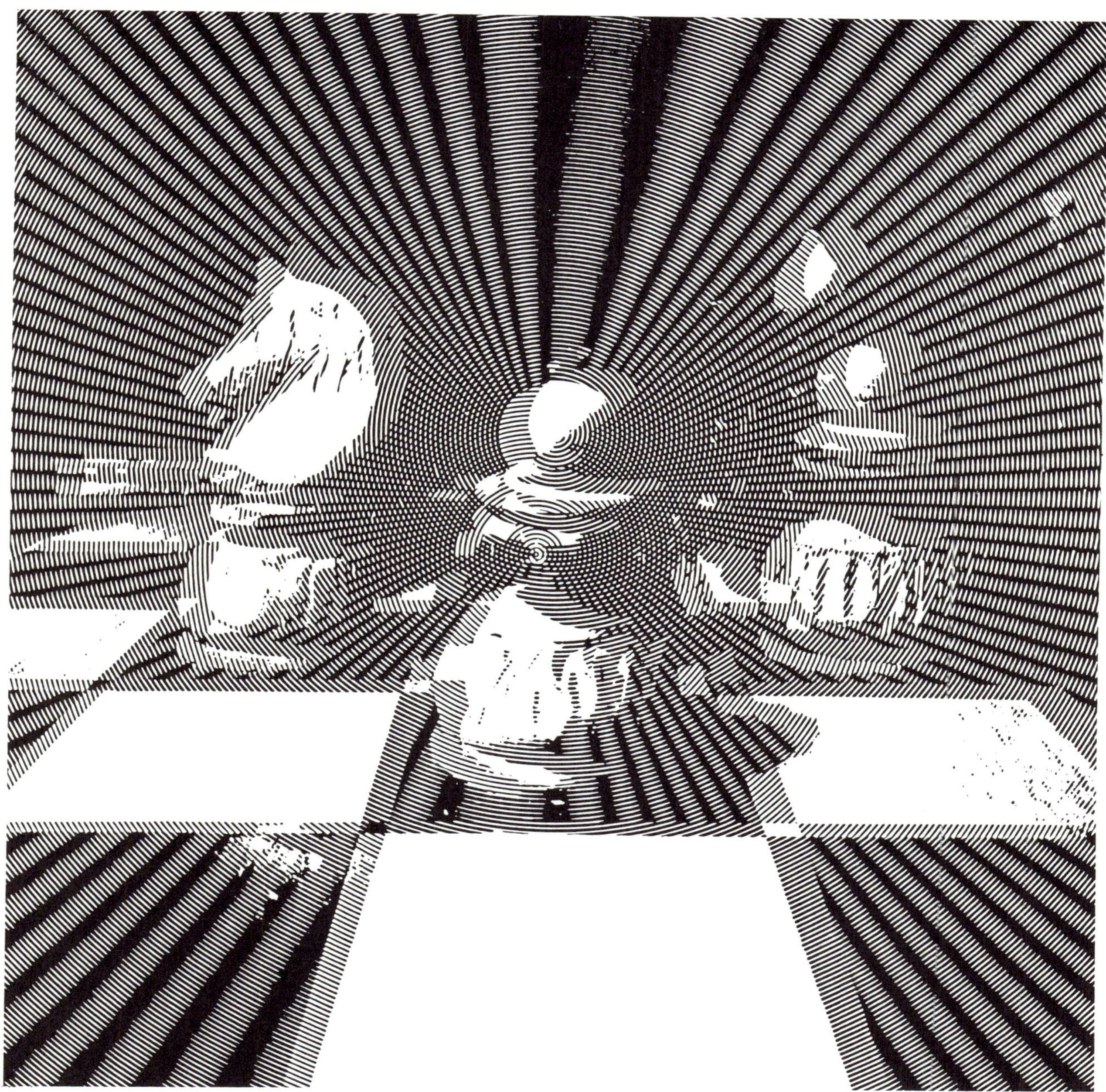

Left. *This technique can best be described as aesthetic experimentation. When separating the image of the dancer into five negatives, one density mask was reversed to positive (the right-hand image). Over a light table, one of the images, plus the reversed one, was positioned and registration hole punched.*

The background area and left figure were printed first with a wiggly line screen in contact with the paper. At the same time a mask was placed under the right-hand figure to retain white in this area.

For the second exposure, a 75 percent gray mezzotint was placed in contact with the paper, and the film containing the right-hand figure was placed in registration and printed. The printing time was the same for both exposures, since each is sufficient to produce black.

Above. *For this cover of a book about chess, a positive color key was placed over the final photo print to create a moiré pattern. In printing, a moiré is caused when the screen angles of the halftones are incorrect. While it is not desirable in reproduction because it interferes with the image, the intentional use of moiré in design can be quite interesting. In this example, the juxtaposition of a circline pattern caused a radiation of lines against circles to a surprising and pleasing effect.*

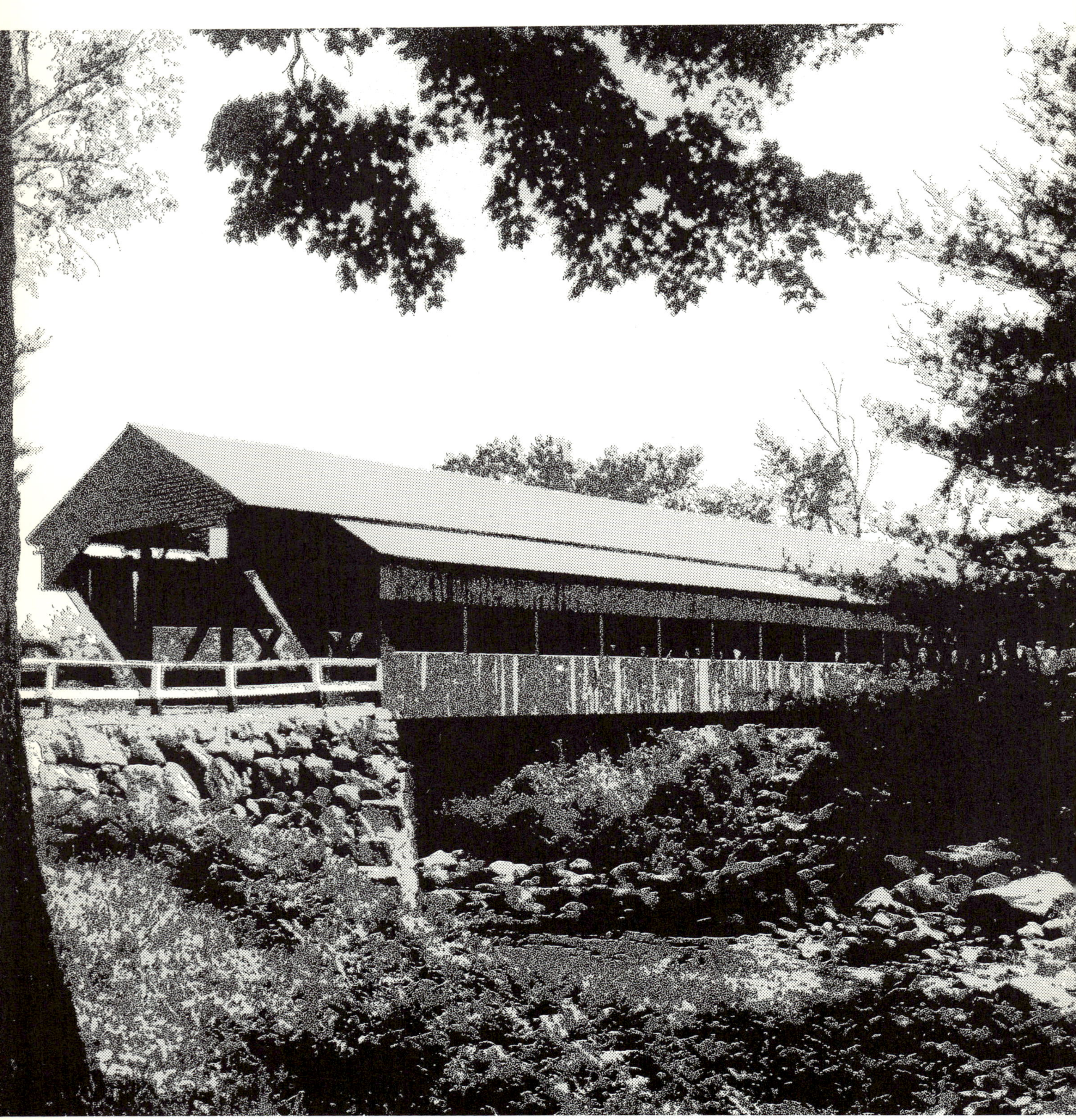

Most posterizations exhibit a hard-edge look. This one has a blending effect, because the mezzotint and light tint help soften the image. White is solid, light gray is a 20 percent dot tint, dark gray is a 50 percent mezzotint, and black is solid.

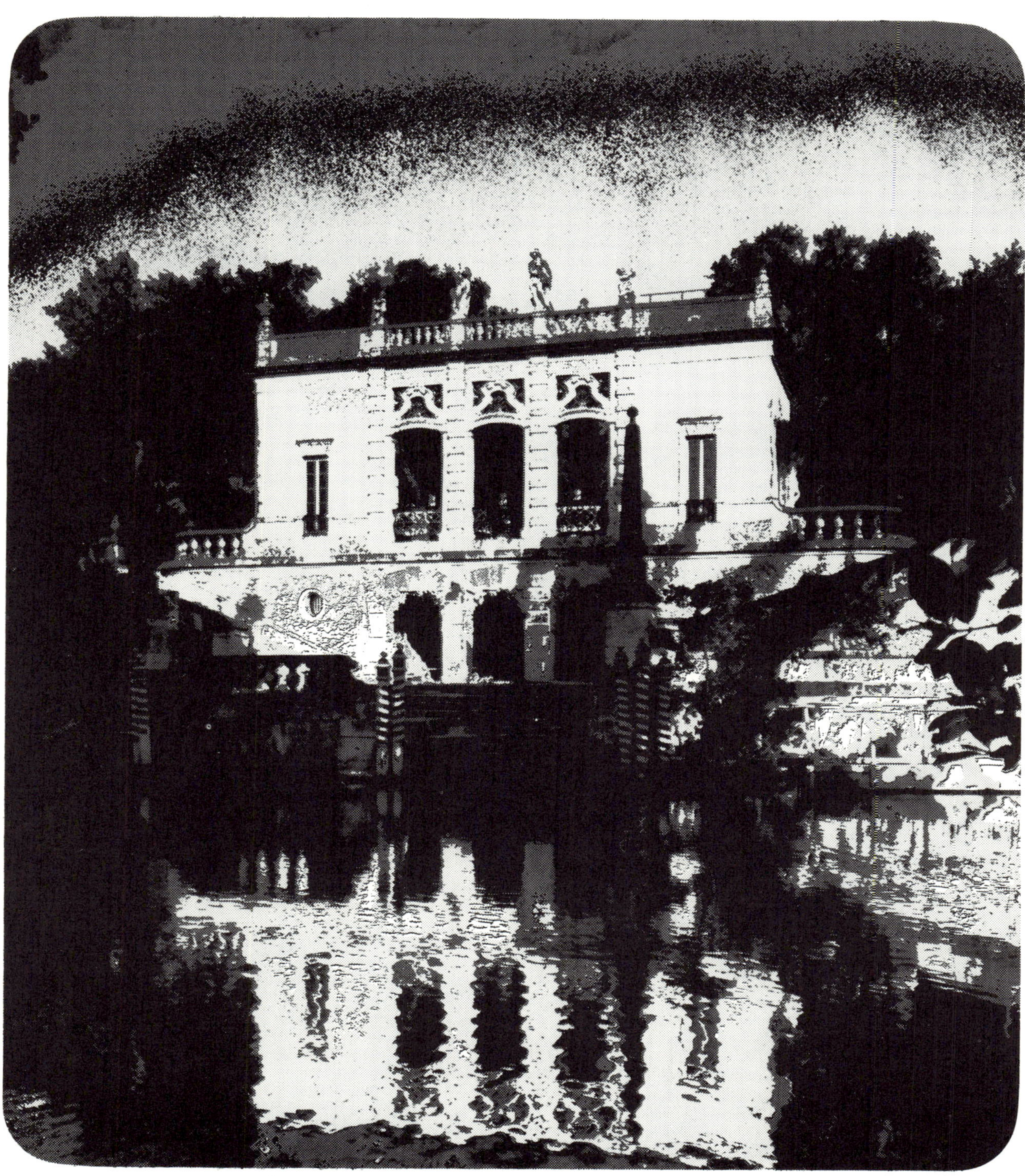

In a number of illustrations in this book, the gray tones were modified by printing through tints. In this one, "Another Time," four-tone posterization was achieved by using two tints in the light and dark areas. For the light-gray simulation, a 25 percent gray, 100-line screen tint (Bychrome) was used. A 60 percent gray, 100-line screen tint was used for the dark-gray area.

A tint in a percentage of gray is a very accurate representation of the dot size for that tone. The designation "100 line" is a measure of the number of dots to the linear inch (2 cm). The master halftone screen through which these tints are made (photographically) has etched lines of 100 to the inch in each direction. The dot is created by exposure, and represents the small area within each square.

Halftone screens vary from 55 lines (coarse) to 150 lines (very fine) to 300 lines (superfine) per inch.

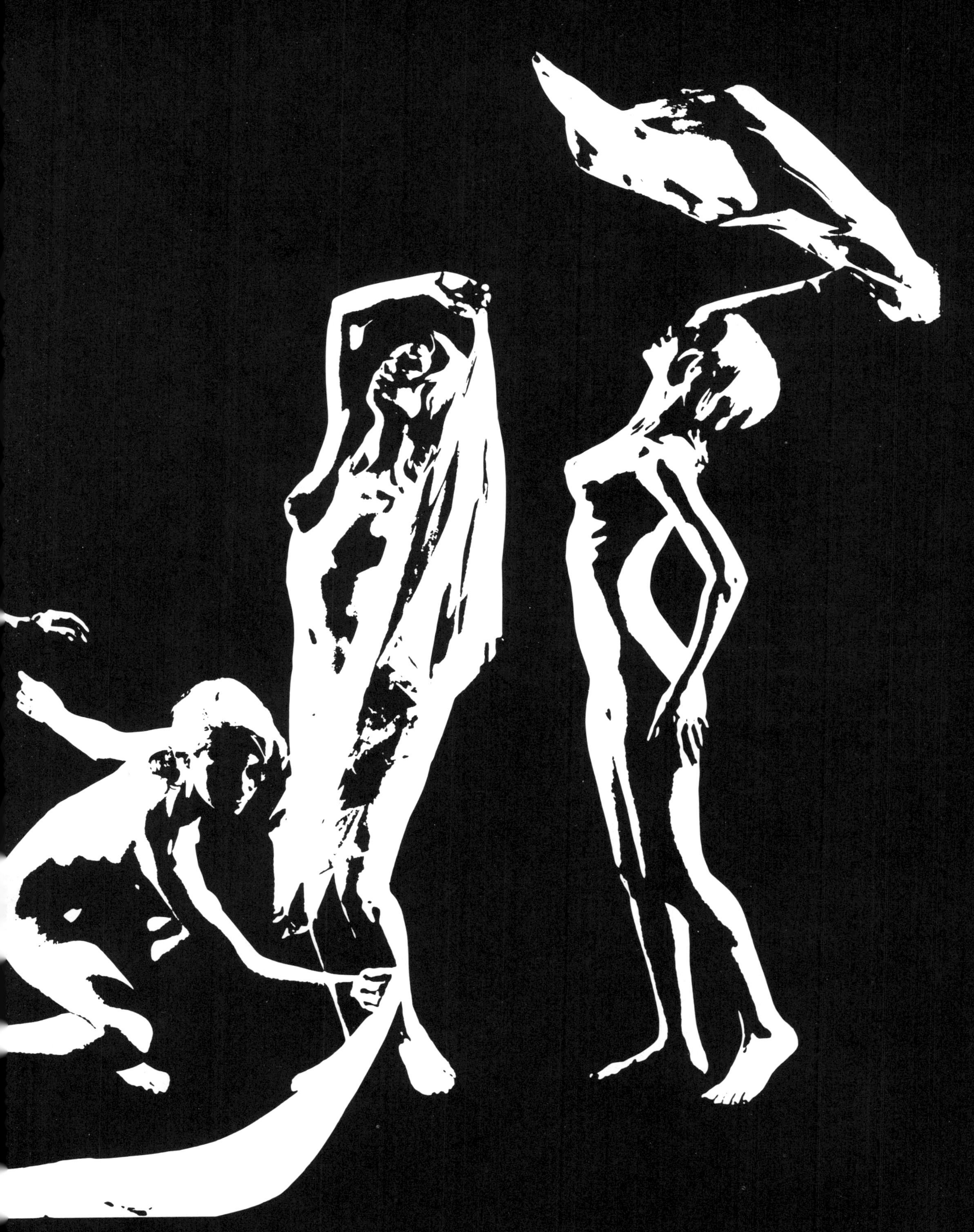